Beyond Bonn

America & the Berlin Republic

by Daniel S. Hamilton

Carnegie Endowment
Study Group on
U.S. Policy toward
Germany
Steven Muller,
Chairman

Design & Production:
Wickham & Associates, Inc.

Copy Editor:
Stephanie Terry

Library of Congress Catalogue Card Number: 94-70056

ISBN: 0-87003-052-3

The Carnegie Endowment for International Peace

The Carnegie Endowment was founded in 1910 by Andrew Carnegie to promote international peace and understanding. To that end the Endowment conducts programs of research, discussion, publication, and education in international affairs and American foreign policy. The Endowment also publishes the quarterly journal *Foreign Policy*.

As a tax-exempt operating foundation, the Endowment maintains a professional staff of Senior and Resident Associates who bring to their work substantial firsthand experience in foreign affairs. Through writing, public and media appearances, congressional testimony, participation in conferences, and other means, the staff engages the major policy issues of the day in ways that reach both expert and general audiences. Accordingly, the Endowment seeks to provide a hospitable umbrella under which responsible analysis and debate may be civilly conducted, and it encourages Associates to write and speak freely on the subjects of their work. The Endowment serves as a forum for discussion, debate, and policy consultation, and from time to time issues reports of commissions or study groups.

The Endowment does not take institutional positions on public policy issues and funds its activities principally from its own resources, supplemented by other non-governmental, philanthropic sources of support.

Carnegie Endowment Officers and Trustees

Contents

7   *Foreword*
    Steven Muller

9   *Introduction*

13   A New Setting—The Berlin Republic

13   Berlin ist nicht Weimar, aber auch nicht Bonn

16   The Berlin Republic's Foreign Policy Orientation

19   American Approaches

19   Pivotal Partners

20   Closing the Expectation Gap

21   The Bilateral Relationship: Motor of Multilateralism

23   Domestic Harmony?

29   New Bargains

33   New Security Bargains

33   The Triangle of Tension
        German Worries

35   A New Strategic Partnership Toward the East
        The Challenge of Ukraine

40   Remaking Collective Defense and Security
        A New NATO
        Putting CSCE to Work
        Flexible Defense

46   Promoting German Strategic Maturity
        Can Germany Participate?
        The Bundeswehr: A Partial Partner?
        The U.S., Germany and the U.N.

53   Redefining Transatlantic Economic Relations

54   Pacific Promises, Atlantic Realities
63   Taking Europe Seriously
        The Need for Flexible Dialogue Mechanisms

65   Coping with Regionalization

67   Widening Transatlantic Economic Relations

69   Deepening the Relationship
        A Transatlantic Investment Code
        Other Microeconomic Compacts

73   Learning and Competitiveness

78   Money Matters

81   A New Vision

83   A Strategic Environmental Initiative

84   A German-American Strategic Partnership

87   A High-Level Environmental Working Group

88   Sorting Out the Right Answers
        Unlocking the Secret of Sustainable Development
        The Environment and Trade
        Cleaner Chemicals
        Investigating the Precautionary Principle

98   *Endnotes*

99   *Participants in the
    Study Group*

101   *Appendix: The North
    Atlantic Treaty*

97   The United States and the Berlin Republic

v

Foreword

United Germany and the United States continue to need each other
for the days ahead. America looks to Europe for an enduring alliance
committed to the advancement of global prosperity, stability and security, and Germany plays a key and—at least at times—determining
role in European affairs. The Federal Republic of Germany, for its
part, looks to the United States as its continuing anchor to windward
in stormy weather—the indispensable resource for German and
European security and stability.

A question is frequently asked whether the future will bring a
European Germany or a German Europe—sometimes followed by
the question of which of these alternatives American policy should
encourage. The obvious answer to both questions is not a simple
choice, but a finely tuned blend of both. The more important—indeed
the crucial—question is whether both the United States and Europe
will remain transatlantic partners. I believe that the welfare of the
planet depends substantially on an affirmative answer. A continued
firm German and American commitment to partnership holds the key
both to the transatlantic alliance and to Germany's future in Europe.

Another question is whether the United States is turning away from
Europe in favor of Asia. To pose an either/or choice in the matter is
foolishness. As the world's lone superpower, America is obliged more
than ever to look around the sweep of the compass. A determined
new look across the Pacific may well be in order—may even be over-
due—but it does not require neglect of Europe. The fact that the Oder-
Neisse line no longer marks the front line of confrontation with the former Soviet Union, as well as burgeoning prosperity in many parts of
Asia, provide the United States with increased freedom and cause to
make a reassessment eastward. But the fragile condition of the newly
independent states once under Soviet hegemony and the deeply rooted market links between America and the European Union suffice to
deny even the possibility that Washington's interest in Europe is on the
wane. A diminution of American Eurocentrism is more virtue than vice
and should not be mislabeled as neglect.

A review and a renewed affirmation of United States policy and
commitment toward the Federal Republic of Germany is timely, and
so I am deeply grateful to the Carnegie Endowment for convening
the Study Group for this purpose and for allowing me the privilege of
the chairmanship. The Study Group managed five intensive meetings

over a span of only eight weeks, and I am much beholden to each participant. We did not attempt to reach consensus on every point under discussion, but we did find ourselves in agreement on the fundamental issues. Dan Hamilton's paper ably reflects the range of our deliberations. He draws on our discussions to formulate his own views. We are all in his debt for this outstanding effort.

Steven Muller
Chairman
Carnegie Endowment Study Group
on U.S. Policy Toward Germany

Introduction

This essay recommends ways to reinvigorate one of America's most important bilateral relationships in light of German unification, radical changes in the European landscape and new domestic and international priorities facing each country. Reshaping policy toward Germany is an essential element of rethinking American policy toward Europe and the U.S. role in the world.

I do not try to identify the lowest common denominator of consensus within the Carnegie Study Group, which in such exercises too often turns out to be mush. Rather I suggest a variety of ways Americans might approach a Germany undergoing a significant transformation. The starting point is to understand that the emerging Berlin Republic will not simply be the Bonn Republic writ large. It also means taking account of the unsettled nature of America's own role in the world.

These challenges notwithstanding, the United States and Germany remain pivotal partners, both to each other and to the international order. The bilateral relationship can serve as a motor for multilateral purposes.

This principle underpins a variety of objectives for the German-American relationship that together make up a new transatlantic bargain.

First is the establishment of a German-American strategic partnership toward central and eastern Europe and the Soviet successor states. This is needed to revamp Europe's collective defense and security organizations, which in turn hinge on active American engagement in Europe and a German commitment to establish the political and operational preconditions to fulfill its part of a new security bargain. Germany must transform itself from an importer to an exporter of security and stability.

If Germans and Americans are prepared to update their security relations, they and their partners must be ready to reinvent transatlantic economic ties as well. The essay outlines seven steps that build transatlantic components into the deepening and widening European Union.

Finally, Germany and the United States are uniquely suited to be promoters of multilateral change on environmental issues. The essay outlines a number of areas for German-American initiatives to mobilize broader coalitions to resolve environmental challenges.

If the relationship is to retain its significance for both countries, it must be based on a common agenda for the future, not a nostalgia for the past. If Germans and Americans are to strike a new transatlantic bargain, business as usual will not suffice.

This essay argues that the United States should engage its German partner energetically on many fronts. German and American interests do not always coincide. But areas of strategic convergence far outweigh those of divergence. Much depends on the time and energy leaders will invest in the relationship. It is an open question.

Each country is captivated by its domestic challenges. Domestic renewal is urgent and self-evident in both countries. But if this becomes a recipe for mutual self-absorption, it poses the greatest challenge to the German-American relationship.

It also means missed opportunities. Collaboration on domestic challenges provides the material for new coalitions. On a range of issues facing each country, such as health care reform, jobs, training workers, fighting drugs and organized crime, coping with immigration and dealing with the possibilities and problems of multicultural societies, there are opportunities to compare different national experiences. Such comparisons may be particularly relevant for the German-American relationship, given the federal nature of both political systems, the complex and dynamic nature of their economies, and the rich network of human ties that exists at almost every level of their societies.

I owe a deep debt of gratitude to the members of the Carnegie Study Group, who offered important insights and valuable suggestions. The vast majority concur with the thrust of the essay. Some may differ with specific conclusions, but they all helped me refine my arguments. A particular note of thanks goes to the chairman of the Study Group, Steven Muller, who steered a steady course as the group navigated some rocky shoals, and who gave us the benefit of his own extensive experience in German-American relations.

I have also benefited from the advice of others, including Zbigniew Brzezinski, Jessica Mathews, Robert Gerald Livingston, Jackson Janes, Charles William Maynes, Anne Heald, C. Randall Henning, Marianne Ginsburg, Konrad von Moltke, Fran Urwin, Roger Dower, William Colglazier, John Campbell, Curtis Moore, Brenda Fisher, Dan Price and a number of officials in the German and U.S. governments whose positions preclude me from mentioning their names. Needless to say, they are not responsible for the conclusions drawn here. I profited from participation in Carnegie's Study Group on U.S.-EC relations, an earlier Atlantic Council Study Group on Germany, and the Endowment's National Commission on America and the New World and the production of its book *Changing Our Ways*. Useful suggestions from those groups find support here. Shane Green, Jonas Weiss, Molly O'Meara, Liz Jasper, Jennifer Little, Chris Henley and Susan Hanafin provided welcome assistance throughout the project. I would also like to thank Morton Abramowitz and my colleagues at the Carnegie Endowment for making this project possible. Finally, a note of thanks to Heidi, Siri and Sean Hamilton who sustain me in all that I do.

Daniel Hamilton

A New Setting—The Berlin Republic

Once again, Germany is the fulcrum of Europe. The nation that used to embody Europe's division finds itself once more *das Land in der Mitte*—both geopolitical pivot and central catalyst to the continent's economic and political revival. The Bonn Republic will be transformed during this decade into the Berlin Republic, Europe's cardinal power.

There is no precedent in this century for a peaceful united Germany. The Berlin Republic is the last and best chance to make it work. Europe's future hinges on its success.

Throughout the unity process former Foreign Minister Hans-Dietrich Genscher sought to allay concerns about a dominant *Deutschland*. "Our aim," he said, "as Thomas Mann wrote as early as 1952, is to create not a German Europe but a European Germany." The reality is likely to be a little of both: a more European Germany in the heart of a more German Europe.

As the Berlin Republic's policy profile emerges, deep continuities bind it to the highly successful structures of the Bonn Republic. Over four decades Bonn was accorded legitimacy by its citizens and its neighbors for its democratic order, its rule of law, and its social market economy. But perhaps the greatest single factor sealing the historical legitimacy of the Basic Law was its validation by the east German people when they finally won the chance to determine their future.

In addition, Chancellor Helmut Kohl assumed huge financial burdens in exchange for east German and Soviet agreement to unification on essentially west German terms. The Berlin Republic is likely to remain a strong federal democracy wedded to a robust capitalist system underpinned by a deep and generous social welfare system—but it will be neither easy nor automatic.

Berlin ist nicht Weimar, aber auch nicht Bonn

The Berlin Republic bears virtually no resemblance to Wilhelminian, Weimar, or Nazi Germany, not to mention the communist German Democratic Republic (GDR). But to assume that the Berlin Republic will be the Bonn Republic writ large ignores the dynamic forces shaping a new democratic Germany.

In fundamental ways the Berlin Republic is similar to its predecessor. But it finds itself in a profoundly different situation. Integrating

THERE IS NO PRECEDENT IN THIS CENTURY FOR A PEACEFUL UNITED GERMANY. THE BERLIN REPUBLIC IS THE LAST AND BEST CHANCE TO MAKE IT WORK. EUROPE'S FUTURE HINGES ON ITS SUCCESS.

more than 16 million people whose material and spiritual experiences were distinct for 45 years, on a freer yet more tempestuous continent, is causing tremendous psychological challenges and social cleavages. It is taxing institutions designed for a different era. Questions have been reopened about the relationships between Germans and their history, between freedom and social justice, between state, citizen and market, and about the aims, uses and obligations of national power. Basic tenets of the country's vaunted social market are under fire. The fierce and far-from-settled debate about when—or even if—much of the government should move from Bonn to Berlin is a reflection of the country's unsettled state. Germany's society, economy, politics and foreign policy are being transformed.

Unification and the tectonic changes of which it was part have handed the Germans a historic opportunity: to define their interests and commitments in ways that demonstrate that Germany has transcended the tragedies of its past and has accepted the responsibilities that accompany its new weight—in short, to show that Europe's pivotal power will neither hide from nor hide behind its past as it charts its future.

The Berlin Republic is better positioned than its predecessor to deal with its challenges. Germany's significance within the west amplifies its influence within the east while its growing influence in the east enhances its ability to shape western institutions and policies.

Yet this new freedom is disorienting. Having given birth to unity, the country is going through a bout of post-partum depression. Despondency and self-doubt abound. These insecurities, in turn, fuel anxiety among Germany's neighbors.

Germans have been stunned to discover that unification is more difficult, costlier, and slower than most had assumed. The difficulties have been exacerbated by an unwillingness or inability to realize that the collapse of the GDR and its subsequent incorporation would create a corresponding crisis of adjustment in western Germany.

While the Germans are now one people constitutionally, they are far from being unified economically, socially or emotionally. It will take at least another decade before the equality of living standards among Germans postulated in the constitution is achieved and at least a generation before the mental barriers between east and west dissipate. These tensions reverberate in Europe.

IT WILL TAKE AT LEAST AN-
OTHER DECADE BEFORE THE
EQUALITY OF LIVING STAN-
DARDS AMONG GERMANS
THAT IS POSTULATED IN THE
CONSTITUTION IS ACHIEVED
AND AT LEAST A GENERATION
BEFORE THE MENTAL BARRI-
ERS BETWEEN EAST AND WEST
DISSIPATE.

Unification initially served to consolidate rather than challenge the political party spectrum that marked the Bonn Republic. During the rapid march to unity the powerful west German political machine dominated the scene. But deeper currents are carving out new channels of change.

For forty years the Bonn Republic fortified itself not only against its external enemies but also against internal challengers. Domestic tranquility was essential to a country astride the fault line of two antagonistic blocs whose own earlier domestic upheavals had been punctuated by wars and hyperinflation. The grave self-doubts harbored by the framers of the Basic Law about the German people's ability to wage democracy coincided with the need to maintain constant vigilence in the battle against communism abroad and those deemed to serve communist interests at home. These doubts and necessities shaped aspects of the Bonn Republic's criminal law, its civil service law, regulations regarding the right of assembly or petition, its approach to law and order, provisions regarding the use of its military abroad, its highly mediated form of representative democracy, and its 5 percent clause governing admission of political parties into the *Bundestag*.

The Bonn Republic's brand of politics fits neither the country's new responsibilities abroad nor its challenges at home. The end of the Cold War threat and the collapse of external borders across Europe have shaken Germany's internal political alignments. Germany's changing position in the global economy has eroded the traditional strongholds of the two major parties—for the Social Democratic Party (SPD) industrial workers linked with trade unions, and for the Christian Democratic Union (CDU) the rural population with strong church ties. A new generation of middle class white collar employees and civil servants is more flexible in its voting behavior. Moreover, the vast majority of east Germans show no clear voting patterns based on social class or traditional party loyalties.

German politics in the 1990s is characterized by pervasive disen-chantment with "politics as usual," relatively low voter turnout (by German standards) in elections, a greater inclination among those who do vote to use the ballot box as an instrument of protest or re-buke, and a greater willingnesss to try new political alternatives than ever would have been demonstrated by the stability-conscious citi-

FLASHES OF GERMAN ASSERTIVENESS ARE AS MUCH A PRODUCT OF WEAKNESS AND DISORIENTATION AS OF CONFIDENCE AND STRENGTH.

zens of the Bonn Republic. These trends provide fresh opportunities for new affiliations inside and outside the conventional party spectrum. They are likely to recast the German political landscape.

The Berlin Republic's Foreign Policy Orientation

The Bonn Republic was a product of the Cold War. Semi-sovereign and dependent on its allies for its security and eventual reunification, it had a habit of thinking of itself as an international lightweight long after it had become a heavyweight. Its overriding foreign policy principles: don't get out in front, don't go it alone. It advanced its national interests in the language of economics and multilateralism and had a narrow view of its alliance obligations: The alliance was there to protect Germany. It was deemed unlikely that Germany would be called on to protect others. Outside the NATO area it could not participate, but it could pay. Checkbook diplomacy bailed the Bonn Republic out of many a jam. A related perception was that military power was a declining asset. The future belonged to "civilian" powers; most crises, it seemed, could be resolved through nonmilitary means.

The Berlin Republic no longer has the antagonistic Soviet superpower or the blood feud across the Wall that defined the Bonn Republic's foreign policy as well as many of its domestic policies. It is finding it harder to hide behind history, multilateralism or the economy.

Multilateralism allowed Bonn to compensate for its partial sovereignty. Sometimes German officials used it to assert their interests; at other times they used it to avoid decisions. Now it no longer provides clear answers in some areas and makes new demands in others. While committed to multilateralism, the German political class is becoming less inhibited about using Germany's new clout to retool old institutions, shape new ones and achieve terms of engagement with major partners more beneficial to their perception of German interests. To apply President Bill Clinton's comments about the United States, Germany will instinctively seek to act together where it can, but is now freer and under greater pressure to act alone where it feels it must.

Europe's turmoil and drift have damaged the German public's confidence in European solutions to national problems. At the same time, the legacy of international reticence, which once facilitated German participation in collective enterprises, now hampers it, for in-

THE BERLIN REPUBLIC IS LIKELY TO BE A MORE OPEN YET LESS SETTLED SOCIETY, ONE MORE VOLATILE POLITICALLY, MORE PRESSURED ECONOMICALLY AND LESS CIRCUMSPECT INTERNATIONALLY THAN THE BONN REPUBLIC TO WHICH GERMANY'S NEIGHBORS AND ALLIES—AND THE GERMANS THEMSELVES— HAD GROWN ACCUSTOMED OVER FORTY YEARS.

stance in peacekeeping operations. Post-Wall events such as the Persian Gulf war and the Bosnian tragedy demonstrate that the luxury of "civilian power" rests on the tenuous assumption that allied "military powers" will guard common interests. The option of checkbook diplomacy is diminishing. Money is tight. Given the staggering costs of unification, all the Germans can do is write hot checks.

As a prime beneficiary of the end of the Cold War, Germany is expected by many neighbors to shoulder considerable burdens of adjustment. The Russians expect their support for unification to be repaid with greater economic assistance and a new special relationship; east European reformers expect aid and blueprints for economic and social modernization; west European partners expect Germany to spearhead the drive toward a deeper and wider European Union (EU); Americans press the Germans to shoulder greater political-military responsibilities and help boost global economic recovery. The historical fear of being dominated by the Germans has been subsumed, it seems, by the even greater fear of being neglected by German capital and German elites.

In important ways, German leaders are seeking to meet these expectations. Yet the concern on the Rhine and the Spree is less the possibility of aggressive *Machtpolitik* than anti-imperial overstretch. United Germany may have no enemies, but it may have too many needy friends. Both the German public and the political class fear a Germany that can't say *Nein*, one so pressed to foot the bill for so many simultaneous commitments that it falls on its head.

In sum, the Berlin Republic is likely to be a more open yet less settled society, one more volatile politically, more pressured economically and less circumspect internationally than the Bonn Republic to which Germany's neighbors and allies—and the Germans themselves—had grown accustomed over forty years. Flashes of German assertiveness are as much a product of weakness and disorientation as of confidence and strength. Much will depend on how well the country is able to consolidate the ongoing process of unification and the assistance and resistance it receives from its primary partners in adjusting to a new role.

American Approaches

How should Americans approach the Berlin Republic? Where do German and American interests coincide, where do they compete and where do they simply diverge? What should we encourage, what should we discourage and why?

When thinking about how to approach the Berlin Republic it would be shallow to concentrate solely on Germany itself. Such a focus ignores a decisive issue for American policy: The United States, the linchpin of the entire international system, is itself one of the biggest question marks on the global scene. At issue are the nature of America's involvement in the world and the balance of attention and resources between domestic and international affairs. We can be more selective about where and how we should be engaged in the new world. But we have no handy guidebook showing us the way.

In both countries the initial euphoria over the crumbling of the Berlin Wall and the peaceful collapse of the Soviet empire has given way to a sober appreciation of the challenges ahead. The new "whirled" order offers no ready answers. There is no sum to its parts. Despite a common yearning for an organizing principle—*ein Gesamtkonzept*—that can provide strategic tidiness, no single doctrine like containment will serve as a guidestar. Moreover, the search for such a slogan is likely to divert energy away from the hard reflection about national interests that is really needed.

Pivotal Partners

A number of considerations can guide policy. There is a solid foundation upon which to build. During the Cold War the United States and the Federal Republic of Germany drew strength and orientation from the other. Each invested heavily and successfully in their relationship. The German-American partnership within the Western alliance has been an exceptional one, shaped under exceptional circumstances. It is testimony to the success of a bipartisan foreign policy created and followed by nine presidents and six chancellors, with deep and consistent support by the publics and leaders of both countries.

The bilateral relationship is the drivewheel of multilateral progress on any major issue in transatlantic relations when Germans and Americans agree, and the brake when they do not. Germany and America remain pivotal partners, both to each other and to the inter-

THE U.S.-GERMAN RELATIONSHIP IS EITHER THE DRIVEWHEEL OR THE BRAKE OF MULTILATERAL PROGRESS ON ANY MAJOR ISSUE IN TRANSATLANTIC RELATIONS.

national order: Few great goals can be achieved by either nation alone, but few great goals can be achieved without the United States and Germany.

The two nations form the core of NATO. They are at the heart of western efforts to consolidate democracy, arms reductions and market reforms in eastern Europe and the Soviet successor states. They are two of the three most important members of the global economic system and its principal coordinating body, the G-7. They are the top two exporters in the world. The dollar and the *Deutsche Mark* are the two principal reserve currencies in the world and the most important currencies in private sector foreign exchange transactions. Americans and Germans are global pacesetters in education, science and innovation. They are leaders both in environmental progress and environmental degradation.

Human ties are deep and extensive. Since 1945 more Americans have lived and worked in Germany than in any other foreign country. Virtually the entire postwar generation of west German leaders has lived, studied or traveled in the United States. A vast web of trade, banking, cultural and educational ties links the two peoples.

Closing the Expectation Gap

Unfortunately, success can breed superficiality. We run the danger of idealizing our role in Germany just as Germans for decades viewed the United States in their own idealized image. If the Berlin Republic is not the Bonn Republic writ large, it is also not America writ small. U.S. expectations of a new and powerful junior partner in the world— one that automatically shares the American worldview, is consistently supportive of American initiatives and is invariably deferential to American sensibilities—are bound to be disappointed.

Recent bilateral tensions over the Gulf war, Bosnia, Iran, interest rates and trade negotiations underscore the point. Germany and the United States have different needs, obligations, and perspectives. There is potential for German-American disagreement over China, the Middle East, peacekeeping missions, monetary matters or investment rules. Defining conditions of the postwar partnership—and American engagement in Europe—have either disappeared or changed fundamentally. Areas of potential and real conflict that had been obscured by the unifying threat are being brought into sharper focus.

IF THE BERLIN REPUBLIC IS NOT THE BONN REPUBLIC WRIT LARGE, IT IS ALSO NOT AMERICA WRIT SMALL.

But the interests that coincide are far weightier than those that do not. The context for U.S. relations with Europe may have changed, but bedrock American interests in Europe endure: a continent free from domination by any power or combination of powers hostile to the United States; prosperous partners open to our ideas, our goods and our investments; a community of shared values, extending across as much of Europe as possible, that can facilitate cooperation with the United States on a growing range of global issues; a continent that is not so wracked by strife that it drains inordinate resources from the United States or the rest of the world. These interests require active U.S. engagement in Europe. They also point to close cooperation with Germany and its European partners.

Germany, too, has vested interests in a democratic, prosperous, outward-looking European Union aligned with the United States; consolidation of democracy, arms reductions and market reforms in eastern Europe and the Soviet successor states; a more effective and efficient international economic order; a more livable world; and the capacity to mobilize collective action to address regional and global issues.

The Bilateral Relationship: Motor of Multilateralism

A fundamental question for U.S. policy toward Germany is the proper relationship between bilateral ties and multilateral efforts. Germany is enmeshed in a dense web of overlapping structures and is a leader in efforts to deepen and extend this network throughout Europe. A strong German-American partnership must be embedded in a more multilateral approach by Washington and Bonn to Europe as a whole.

At the same time, Germany will be the most important actor making sure multilateralism works in Europe. So the bilateral relationship can serve as a motor for multilateral goals. The following chapters suggest German-American initiatives that can actively draw in other partners, provide the intellectual groundwork for future action, and mobilize the broader coalitions that will be needed to address major tasks. That this will be difficult is certain; that it not become an excuse for inaction is imperative.

The European Union will continue to play an important role as a prosperous, democratic home for Germany and as an anchor of stability for eastern Europe. A Germany embedded in a strong

GERMANY WILL BE THE MOST IMPORTANT ACTOR MAKING SURE MULTILATERALISM WORKS IN EUROPE. THE BILATERAL RELATIONSHIP CAN SERVE AS A MOTOR FOR MULTILATERAL GOALS.

European Union within a robust Atlantic Community can generate economic growth and political stability. Failure of the Union would weaken the North American link to Europe. A dominant and perhaps insecure *Deutschland* in a fractious Europe unhinged from America could be a source of conflict. Such a Europe, plagued by xenophobia and protectionism, would evoke memories of its violent past rather than possibilities for a vibrant post-Soviet future.

The significance of the EU for Germany is in turn dependent to a far greater degree than is generally acknowledged on the continuing viability of NATO and Germany's relationship to the United States. The American connection reassures the Germans against events spinning out of control in eastern Europe. The EU is ill-equipped to respond to such challenges on its own. The U.S. presence also reassures Germany's neighbors, who are watching closely German efforts to redefine its role. When Germany acts together with the United States it can do much it cannot do alone. NATO remains essential to Germany as the single functioning multilateral defense mechanism in Europe, as a complement to the EU as an anchor of European stability, and as a forum for coordination among diverse democracies on a broad range of policy issues. The U.S. position also gives Germany a voice in nuclear planning it would not have otherwise.

In short, Germany's commitment to current multilateral arrangements is related to the perception that the United States remains committed to multilateral diplomacy. Temptations toward American unilateralism or withdrawal from European affairs are increasingly significant in this context.

If a new longer term vision for the bilateral relationship is to be found within multinational frameworks, the major European and North Atlantic organizations must be adapted to the new realities of Europe. In addition, transatlantic ties need reinforcement through a strengthened web of "dialogue mechanisms" and ad hoc arrangements. Possibilities are outlined in Chapter Four. German initiatives in this regard should be welcomed by the United States as an important sign that the Berlin Republic is assuming a broader view of its international responsibilities.

Here again a note of caution: Efforts to use Germany to promote the U.S. role in Europe can lead to charges that Germany is acting as a stalking horse for U.S. interests, much as Great Britain was ac-

IMPROVING THE FRANCO-
AMERICAN RELATIONSHIP
MIGHT BE THE SINGLE MOST
IMPORTANT CONTRIBUTION
WASHINGTON COULD MAKE
TO THE GERMAN-AMERICAN
RELATIONSHIP.

cused during its efforts to join the European Community in the early 1960s. One way to dampen such suspicions is to develop a more productive relationship with France. Given Germany's intimate ties with both Paris and Washington, continuing French and American tendencies to define security and economic arrangements in zero-sum terms force the Germans to play an impossible middle role that generates resentments from its two partners and mixed signals from Bonn. Improving the Franco-American relationship might be the single most important contribution Washington could make to the German-American relationship.

Such efforts assume an additional importance given the reality of a deeper and wider European Union. German-American disagreements will inevitably stem from Germany's obligations to its European partners and its commitment to the Union. German commercial and trade policies, for instance, are increasingly made in Brussels. The Uruguay Round of the General Agreement on Tariffs and Trade (GATT) was jeopardized when Germany and its other EU partners failed to rein in French demands.

A common European Union foreign policy, if it is to come at all, remains at sufficient remove in time that the United States must continue to deal with a sovereign united Germany that has considerable freedom to maneuver in foreign policy. But Washington needs to understand better the constraints that Germany's multilateral framework imposes.

Domestic Harmony?

Strengthening the German-American partnership begins at home, whether that home is Berlin or Boston, Los Angeles or Leipzig. This is a cliché, of course, but it has the advantage of being true. It has also taken on new relevance: In both countries the case for domestic renewal is urgent and self-evident. It is an essential foundation for, not an alternative to, an active foreign policy.

We will only be able to act together abroad if we get our acts together at home. An America that lacks economic strength and social cohesion will not be respected abroad. A Germany overwhelmed by the psychological and material costs of unification is unlikely to play the broader global role American policy seeks. If our domestic problems go unaddressed, our capacity to take necessary actions inter-

**IN BOTH COUNTRIES
THE CASE FOR DOMESTIC
RENEWAL IS URGENT
AND SELF-EVIDENT. BUT A
"DOMESTIC FIRST" POLICY
IS A RECIPE FOR
SELF-ABSORPTION.
THIS IS GOING TO BE THE
GREATEST CHALLENGE
FACING THE GERMAN-
AMERICAN RELATIONSHIP.**

nationally will diminish. The world will be both more dangerous and less prosperous. Germans and Americans would turn inward or be tempted to find external scapegoats for problems made in Germany or America. There are already worrisome signs in each country.

But neither Germany nor America can afford to stay home alone. Domestic renewal in each country depends on active engagement abroad. The affairs of the world have become too deeply woven into the fabric of German and American life for either to ignore the rest of the globe while it concentrates on domestic priorities. A "domestic first" policy narrows the domestic consensus within which foreign policy must operate. It is a recipe for self-absorption.

This is going to be the greatest challenge facing the German-American relationship during the next few years. Germans and Americans are each more captivated by their domestic challenges than at any time during the past four decades. Officials and elites in each nation, preoccupied with their own headaches, may resort more frequently to actions designed to address domestic concerns without adequate consideration of their international repercussions. German-American relations could be reduced to the lowest common denominator of domestic necessities. We risk ending up like an old married couple, each of whom sporadically remembers the good old days but gradually forgets why they are still together.

At the same time domestic challenges offer new possibilities. Particularly during times of flux domestic agendas drive foreign policies. On a range of issues facing each country there is an opportunity to use and compare different national experiences. Each country faces problems unique to its national situation, but it is too glib to ignore commonalities—and thus miss opportunities—by focusing narrowly on cultural differences.

Take health care, for example. The German system offers coverage to all yet Germans spend only about half as much per person on health care as Americans do, and the American system leaves 38 million people uninsured. Here is an opportunity to learn.

Common themes emerge as both countries restructure. One is the need to strike a better balance between personal security and flexibility so as to enable working people in each country to adapt to the relentless change that accompanies a competitive open economy. German leaders are trying to give their social market economy the flexibility it needs to remain competitive; the Clinton Administration seeks to provide a base of domestic security that allows American workers to cope with the realities of the global market. Each can offer the other some important guidelines along the way.

Each society provides a frame of reference for the other. Viewing the relationship in this way opens a variety of areas in which deeper German-American collaboration can be mutually beneficial. Both countries face similar challenges: tackling health care reform, creating jobs, training workers, fighting drugs and organized crime, coping with immigration, and dealing with the possibilities and problems of multi-cultural societies. Collaboration on these domestic challenges would help the two partners avoid working at cross purposes or duplicating efforts. It offers opportunities to make more efficient use of scarce polit-ical and economic resources. It provides the material for new coalitions. It also means taking better advantage of contributions that can be

Chart 1

Economic Indicators of Selected Countries

Country	GDP per head $ PPP^a 1991	GDP annual avg % 1983–92	Inflation anuual avg % 1983–92	Unemploy-ment % of labor force– 1992	Total tax as % of GDP 1991	Public sector as % of total employment 1991
United States	22,130	2.7	3.8	7.4	27	14.4
Switzerland	21,780	2.0	3.2	2.5	32	11.0
Germany	19,770	2.7	2.2	7.7	39	15.1
Japan	19,390	4.1	1.8	2.2	30	6.0
Canada	19,320	2.8	4.4	11.3	36	19.7
Hong Kong	18,520	6.3	7.8	2.0	11	6.8
France	18,430	2.2	4.4	10.2	41	22.6
Sweden	17,490	1.7	6.7	5.3	50	31.7
Italy	17,040	2.4	7.4	10.7	31	15.5
Great Britain	16,340	2.2	5.5	10.1	36	19.2
Spain	12,670	3.2	7.6	18.4	35	14.1
South Korea	8,320	9.2	5.1	2.4	16	4.2
Mexico	7,170	1.4	59.2	3.2	18	6.1
Russia	6,930	-2.0	54.6	0.8	40*	98.0*
Hungary	6,080	-0.6	15.2	12.2	50*	20.0*
Brazil	5,240	1.9	472.0	5.9	75	4.5
China	1,680	9.4	8.2	2.3	45*	20.0*
India	1,150	5.2	9.3	11.7	14	8.0*

Note: In all tables German figures refer to all of Germany where available; Russian figures refer to the former Soviet Union in most cases

Sources: The Economist; World Bank; IMF; OECD; ILO; PlanEcon: EIU; IMD; ECLAC; UNDP; UNEP.

* Estimate

^{a} Purchasing-power parity

made outside of government. During the Cold War, national government was the agent of change. It organized a vast national effort to
prevail and prosper in a global military/ideological competition. In a
new era marked by economic competition and information richness,
national government is often ill-equipped to be the primary agent of
change. Other actors, whether private entities or smaller governments such as states, may be more relevant. New networks outside
national governments will carry the relationship.

Such networks are important because much of the human network
built during the past half-century was justified and perpetuated by
the common security threat. As that threat dissipates, old networks
crumble. New coalitions built on common challenges must supple-
ment and gradually supplant old coalitions built on external threats.
Pathos will not hold the relationship together.

This points to a more important role for cultural diplomacy. Both

Chart 2

Social Indicators
of Selected Countries

Country	Second-ary school enrollment rate %[a] 1990	Life expect-ancy at birth, years, 1991	Infant mortality per 1,000 life births, 1991	Doctors per 100,000 people 1990	Pop. density: people per 1,000 hectares 1991	Murder per 100,000 men 1990[b]	Divorce as % of marriages 1990[b]
United States	92	76	9	238	275	13.3	48
Switzerland	85	78	7	159	1,701	1.4	33
Germany	97	76	7	270	2,286	1.0	30
Japan	96	79	5	164	3,294	0.7	22
Canada	99*	77	7	222	29	2.5	43
Hong Kong	90	78	7	93	58,121	1.7	12
France	99	77	7	286	1,036	1.3	31
Sweden	91	78	6	270	209	1.7	44
Italy	79	77	8	476	1,963	3.6	8
Great Britain	84	75	7	164	2,382	1.0	41
Spain	90*	77	8	357	781	1.2	8
South Korea	87	70	16	73	4,435	1.3	11
Mexico	53	70	36	81	452	30.7	8
Russia	80	69	20	476	87	16.3	42
Hungary	79	70	16	294	1,141	3.7	31
Brazil	39	66	58	93	179	29.4	3
China	48	69	38	99	1,255	1.0	1*
India	44	60	90	41	2,902	5.0	1*

Sources: The Economist; World Bank; UNDP; The Economist; "World in Figures"; WHO; IMD.

* Estimate

[a] Secondary school pupils as % of all 12–17-year-olds

[b] Or latest available

partners worked mightily to increase channels of communication during the past half-century. But what do we communicate, what values, what substance? Do we understand each other? Probably to a decreasing extent. Swift means of travel and communication can simply mean that misunderstandings and prejudice travel more rapidly than they did twenty years ago. An offhand statement by a president, a chancellor, the head of the Federal Reserve or the *Bundesbank* is flashed at the speed of light throughout the world. Human reality is reduced to five-second bursts of sound that frequently bite. The results are often confusing; at times they can be catastrophic.

Distance, cultural differences and varying national perspectives mean that currents of ignorance, prejudice and misunderstanding will continue to swirl within a vast sea of information. The very closeness of the German-American relationship makes it especially vulnerable to such misunderstandings. The information age makes the communication of words and ideas more critical. But talking and meeting are

Chart 3

Cultural Indicators of Selected Countries

Country	TVs per 1,000 people 1990	Cinemas per million people 1991[a]	Daily newspapers per 1,000 people 1988–90	Foreign visitors as % of resident population 1991[a]
United States	815	80	250	16
Switzerland	407	59	463	540
Germany	570	47	390	22
Japan	620	15	587	3
Canada	641	28	228	135
Hong Kong	274	29	632	107
France	406	89	210	96
Sweden	474	135	533	30*
Italy	424	62	107	95
Great Britain	435	31	395	31
Spain	396	46	82	137
South Korea	210	16	280	7
Mexico	139	27	127	8
Russia	283	580	400*	3
Hungary	410	100	261	323
Brazil	213	9	54	1
China	31	13	30*	2
India	32	15	28	0.2

Sources: *The Economist*; World Bank; UNDP; Statesman's Yearbook; OECD.

* Estimate

[a] Or last available

IN A NEW ERA MARKED BY ECONOMIC COMPETITION AND INFORMATION RICHNESS, NATIONAL GOVERNMENT IS OFTEN ILL-EQUIPPED TO BE THE PRIMARY AGENT OF CHANGE. OTHER ACTORS, WHETHER PRIVATE ENTITIES OR SMALLER GOVERNMENTS SUCH AS STATES, MAY BE MORE RELEVANT.

not enough. What is said is usually not as important as what is heard.

This means we need to spend more time as interpreters, less in terms of language—although that is more important than ever—than in conveying an understanding of the tremendous transformations affecting each society and how those changes may affect the way members of the one society view the other. After all, the key to one's view of one's partner is the changing view one has of oneself.

Much is being done already. Organizations such as the German Marshall Fund, the American Council on Germany, the Atlantik-Brücke, the American Institute for Contemporary German Studies, the German Studies Association, the Congressional Study Group on Germany, the American Association of Teachers of German, the Aspen Institute Berlin, Inter Nationes, the Goethe Institute, the German political foundations, scores of other foundations and hundreds of schools, universities and other organizations offering study and exchange programs are evidence of binding ties.

Germany has been very active in this area. Initiatives such as the establishment of Centers of Excellence in German and European Studies at Georgetown University, Harvard University and the University of California; Chancellor's Fellowships to promising young Americans through the Alexander von Humboldt Foundation; and the formation of a binational German-American Academic Council are evidence of a firm commitment by the German government, and a personal commitment by Chancellor Kohl, to deepen the relationship.

But more can and should be done. Particular emphasis should be given to east German–American exchanges. Sixteen million east Germans have known the United States only in a systematically distorted way for two generations. Relatively few have studied or speak English. Engaging them in a deeper understanding of American society, values and foreign policy is a vital challenge for the future. Publicly and privately sponsored student and professional exchange programs should facilitate relations between east Germans and Americans, and American universities should be encouraged to establish study abroad programs with east German universities. Should economic realities inhibit expansion of total German-American programs in this area, the east German component should be given preferential treatment for some years to come.

Both the United States and Germany are federal republics. A rich area to explore is the relationship between individual American states and the German *Länder*, not just because it offers another avenue to expand human ties but because so much of the future agenda is concerned with how regions and localities deal with the consequences of global change.

The information, transportation and technology revolutions mean that international events more directly affect local and regional actors than ever before. Regions are able to play a more independent role in international affairs as well. The new global economy not only offers new challenges to relations between nations, it could exacerbate tensions between regional and national authorities. It also offers new opportunities to regional leaders within each nation to form new and profitable coalitions with like-minded regional leaders in other nations to share experiences and address common issues.

An "international regional agenda" is emerging that pushes regions within nations to examine how other regions, rather than other nations, are dealing with three issues: a) the reconciliation of economic growth with regional environmental quality; b) the relationship between learning, technology and competitiveness; and c) such social consequences of internationalization as migration, ethnic diversity, AIDS, drugs, and organized crime. In each area regions are affected directly and immediately. In the United States and Germany they often have greater legal and substantive competence than national authorities to deal with the issues. They already bypass national authorities to attract investment and promote trade. On so-called "intermestic" issues, there is a role in both countries for regional *Nebenaussenpolitik*.

The National Governors' Association and the German *Bundesrat* should be encouraged to facilitate regular meetings and exchanges between American governors and the minister-presidents of the German *Länder*. Previous experiences in developing German-American relations at the state level have been productive. They can be expanded.

New Bargains

The German-American relationship can be advanced in many ways. In the end it is a question of political priority. This essay argues that the United States should engage its German ally energetically on many fronts. In some areas German-American initiatives are likely to advance U.S. interests more effectively than could unilateral approaches or separate action with other partners. In other areas American engagement can prevent real disagreements with Germany from blocking necessary action.

The themes that have been outlined above lead to three principles that should guide relations between the United States and the Berlin Republic.

First, the United States remains Germany's irreplaceable global partner. There is no substitute for American leadership. The United States is the only nation engaged in Europe without a residual fear of Germany. It can maintain a frank and friendly relationship less burdened by mistrust, while at the same time providing a reassuring counterbalance to those nervous about Germany's enhanced weight. It will be a natural partner when it comes to nudging the Berlin Republic toward roles and responsibilities in global political and strategic matters commensurate with its economic and monetary strength.

Second, that leadership must be of a different kind—working with our German ally to build coalitions of the willing. This means a greater German voice as well as greater German burdens. It means changing the way we conduct our affairs. Washington should not count on automatic German support on every issue, but it also need not interpret every hesitation as a sign of anti-Americanism.

Third, if domestic challenges and generational change are not used as an opportunity to build new coalitions, they are likely to become a recipe for mutual indifference. The relationship is strong, but it cannot be taken for granted.

These three principles underpin three broad objectives for the German-American relationship that are described in the following chapters. Together they constitute a new transatlantic bargain.

To strike a new security bargain we must

- **Form a German-American strategic partnership** to consolidate democracy, arms reductions and market reforms in central and eastern Europe and the Soviet successor states;

- **Remake Europe's collective security organizations** and create new relationships between them;

- **Promote a broader German strategic perspective.**

To strike a new economic bargain we must

- **Build transatlantic components into the deeper and wider European Union** through a range of
  - flexible "dialogue mechanisms;"
  - dispute-dampening and market-opening arrangements; and
  - microeconomic and monetary compacts that expand global trade and promote growth.

To strike a new environmental bargain we must

- **Form a strategic partnership on the environment** that

  - generates the political momentum for a high-level U.S.-EU working group on the environment;

  - confronts issues where the challenge is not to generate the political will to take widely agreed upon actions, but where the right answers are not yet clear, for example in the tradeoffs involved in
    - sustainable development;
    - trade and the environment;
    - cleaner chemicals;
    - scientific uncertainty vs. the possibility of irreversible global change.

New Security Bargains

During the Cold War the United States was central to a security order in Europe that contained Soviet power, provided a secure and positive framework for German energies, muted far older European conflicts, and shaped conditions that promoted intense and fruitful collaboration among west European nations. The United States, in the words of one analyst, became Europe's pacifier.

As long as the armed truce of the Cold War seemed secure, there appeared to be little need for any serious reconsideration of the underlying premises of European or American security policies. These underpinnings have now been fundamentally altered, as have the security challenges that face the United States and Europe.

The Triangle of Tension

While direct challenges from Eurasia to America's physical security are fewer than at any time since the 1930s, Europe and America face a triangle of tension that threatens stability, democracy and prosperity on the continent and thus impinges on U.S. vital interests. The first leg of the triangle is Russia itself. The second is a zone of instability extending through eastern Europe to Russia's rim. The third spans the Mediterranean, Northern Africa and the Middle East.

The spectrum of risks generated within this triangle is wide-ranging: wars and civil wars generated by territorial ambition, ethnic and religious hatreds; genocidal policies; the collapse of state and social order; the economic and social impoverishment of whole regions; the possibility of nuclear power accidents and other environmental dangers; and the proliferation of weapons of mass destruction and modern weapons technology in places where aggression is still a considered means of politics.

All of these risks threaten civilian populations. All threaten nascent democracies in the region. All threaten to spill over into the West in the form of terrorism and refugees. Some threaten to draw major powers onto opposite sides. Some mock the credibility of both rhetorical and formal western commitments to basic human rights and fundamental freedoms. They remind us of the fragility of post–Cold War peace. And all render obsolete the alliance's traditional distinction between "in" and "out" of area.

EUROPE AND AMERICA FACE A TRIANGLE OF TENSION THAT THREATENS STABILITY, DEMOCRACY AND PROSPERITY ON THE CONTINENT AND THUS IMPINGES ON U.S. VITAL INTERESTS. THE FIRST LEG OF THE TRIANGLE IS RUSSIA ITSELF. THE SECOND IS A ZONE OF INSTABILITY EXTENDING THROUGH EASTERN EUROPE TO RUSSIA'S RIM. THE THIRD TIER SPANS THE MEDITERRANEAN, NORTHERN AFRICA AND THE MIDDLE EAST.

These risks cannot adequately be confronted by a purely military approach to security issues, and either they will be dealt with collectively or they will not be dealt with at all.

German Worries

These challenges are particularly important to Germany. The Wall may have come down, but Germany is still thinking of itself as a front-line state, one less threatened than frightened by the east.

Following unification and the collapse of the Soviet Union Germany is faced with an epochal shift in its strategic priorities. For almost half a century the Bonn Republic's strategic imperative was to overcome the division of Europe, to enmesh itself within the west, to prove it was a stable democracy, and to solidify both the Franco-German and the American-German partnerships. It has achieved those goals. For the next half–century Germany's strategic imperative has shifted eastward. Relations with the west remain essential, but in relation to a very different strategic priority: to consolidate democracy, arms reductions and market economies as far eastward as possible. Surrounded by friendly, prosperous and above all stable democracies, the Berlin Republic might finally escape the historically tragic dilemma of Germany's *Mittellage* straddling East and West.

In the post-Wall world Germany's number one security threat is no longer a massive invasion across the central European plain, it is the aftershocks of the political and economic earthquakes that have shaken the east and that threaten to spill into the west in the form of mass migration, xenophobia, economic dislocation, secessionist movements and regional instability, perhaps drawing the Germans into ethnic or nationalist conflicts as patrons of endangered German minorities or as a base from which extremist groups could fuel bitter ethnic struggles, terrorism and nuclear proliferation. These dangers could destroy a historic opportunity to consolidate democracy and market-based economic reforms throughout Europe and damage the habits of cooperation that west European nations have built up over more than four decades. Such concerns are driving much of German foreign policy.

German officials are concerned that their sense of urgency is insufficiently appreciated by their western partners. If the west dithers in response to eastern turmoil there will be enormous pressures on

THESE RISKS CANNOT ADE-
QUATELY BE CONFRONTED BY
A PURELY MILITARY AP-
PROACH TO SECURITY ISSUES,
AND EITHER THEY WILL BE
DEALT WITH COLLECTIVELY OR
THEY WILL NOT BE DEALT
WITH AT ALL.

Germany to dilute its multilateral instincts with a range of bilateral and unilateral endeavors to channel this process of chaotic change. If common efforts fail to keep pace with the German sense of urgency, Germany will feel compelled to act alone, contrary to its clear prefer- ences and its own best interests. The German decision to recognize Croatia and Slovenia and Germany's bilateral migration agreements with east European countries are only the most visible expressions of these underlying pressures, underscoring Germany's yearning for stability as well as its new willingness to use its clout if necessary— and not always with advantageous results.

Germany will be preoccupied with the east. But the collective east European, Baltic, Russian and Ukrainian *Drang nach Westen* is much more relevant to contemporary Europe than older ghosts of a German *Drang nach Osten*. German policy is driven by concerns about solvency and stability, not dreams of domination.

Over half of all western assistance to eastern Europe and the Soviet successor states has come from German sources. The fact that much of this assistance consists either of payments to the Russians in exchange for unity or subsidies tied to Russian orders that keep otherwise uncompetitive east German firms afloat does not diminish the German contribution as much as it indicates the close connections German leaders perceive between reforms in the east- crn half of the continent and Germany's sense of security.

A New Strategic Partnership Toward the East

As this new orientation begins to form, the United States stands as the only other country that potentially has the vision, the will, the wal- let and an equivalent sense of urgency to join forces with Germany. There is a vital strategic convergence between the two countries with regard to eastern Europe, Russia and a number of other Soviet suc- cessor states such as Ukraine. This can and should be translated into a strategic partnership that acts as the drivewheel of progress to export democratic structures, assist market-oriented reforms, secure arms reductions, develop habits of military cooperation and promote civilian control of the military throughout eastern Europe and the Soviet successor states while facilitating their association and even- tual integration into western structures. Other nations have to be in- cluded, but the bilateral relationship will be the essential fulcrum of

FOR THE NEXT HALF—CENTURY GERMANY'S STRATEGIC IMPERATIVE HAS SHIFTED EASTWARD.

change. Such efforts could do more to enhance European security than a narrow focus on purely military security.

A U.S. commitment to such a partnership could also ward off potential German-American differences regarding central and eastern Europe on the one hand, and Russia and Ukraine on the other. As the west considers how and whom to draw into its structures, most in western Europe and many in Germany would prefer to start drawing some lines separating those who are "in" and those who are "out." Europe, they say, should end where the real trouble begins: Russia and Ukraine.

The problems of the east, particularly those of Russia and Ukraine, are potentially overwhelming. They certainly are too vast to be affected significantly by any single outside nation operating alone or apart. But it would be folly to draw a new curtain a few hundred kilometers east of the old one. If Russia moves fitfully in ways conducive to western interests, we should not exclude it from western structures. The United States should make it clear that western support of eastern reforms cannot stop at the eastern border of Poland. Washington should be engaged fully in joint efforts, particularly with Germany, to ensure that those reforms succeed.

Ultimately, successful reforms will have to come from within. But a German-American strategic partnership can help. Normally, outside forces are likely to exert only a marginal influence on a large nation, such as Russia. But during such a period of great transformation, outside influence can make a difference. The surprising parliamentary showing of Vladimir Zhirinovsky and his neo-fascists underscores three facts about the second Russian revolution: A wide range of outcomes are still possible; events there will have a profound effect on the outside world; and western action or inaction will be crucial.

Moreover, American participation facilitates German actions with east Europeans and Russians who are mindful of history. East Europeans are eager to return to Europe, but they have also shown themselves to be enthusiastic supporters of a transatlantic tie. The United States can play a vital role as geopolitical equalizer and benign arbiter for those countries harboring residual fears of their neighbors. It can help Germany be a catalyst for reform in a way other nations cannot.

THE SURPRISING PARLIAMENTARY SHOWING OF VLADIMIR ZHIRINOVSKY AND HIS NEO-FASCISTS UNDERSCORES THREE FACTS ABOUT THE SECOND RUSSIAN REVOLUTION: A WIDE RANGE OF OUTCOMES ARE STILL POSSIBLE; EVENTS THERE WILL HAVE A PROFOUND EFFECT ON THE OUTSIDE WORLD; AND WESTERN ACTION OR INACTION WILL BE CRUCIAL.

Germany, in turn, can amplify U.S. efforts through its own extensive contacts, its political acumen, its economic resources and its understanding that "security" involves more than the military. Without Germany it will prove impossible to integrate east Europeans and Russians into western structures. Without Germany these countries are unlikely to recover economically.

As part of the partnership Germany and America should make concerted efforts to identify the problems, to construct policies toward the countries of the east that take account of each other, to harmonize national policies as appropriate, to hammer out initiatives that can be taken bilaterally and to use the bilateral relationship to build a broader consensus for action among the club of democracies. The key is to work together to *understand* the situation so sound joint policies can result. Ambassador Strobe Talbott's November visit to Bonn and Vice President Al Gore's mid-December meeting with Chancellor Kohl are good first steps. But more can be done. The danger of doing too little too late remains high.

Such a partnership would involve a mixture of bilateralism and multilateralism infused with a strategic view. It should and can be pursued in a way that recognizes Germany's commitments to the European Union. For example, the two nations could work out an initiative that could then be submitted to the EU to increase east European access to western markets by lowering import quotas in key areas such as textiles, agriculture and steel. This could be tied to U.S. willingness to provide greater access to its markets.

The U.S. government initiative of "enterprise funds" under private-sector management to spur the creation of small and medium-sized private enterprises could be strengthened by adding German partners. Both countries could extend investment tax credits to companies that set up operations in Russia and Ukraine. Other willing governments could join such initiatives.

Targeted efforts to achieve tangible improvements in the daily lives of the Russian people could blunt demogogic appeals. It is important to shift aid from the central government toward regions and local organizations. One approach might be a German-American initiative to launch a broader multilateral fund to establish and strengthen social safety nets for regions and local governments undergoing painful reforms. With help from the fund and national governments, German *Länder*, American states and non-governmental institutions might join forces with those in other western countries to lend "know how" technical assistance to Russian partner regions and organizations.

Joint German-American "Democracy Houses" in Soviet successor states could be established that build on the tradition set by the 50 America Houses the United States established in Germany after World War II.

German and American foundations are primary external catalysts of reform in eastern Europe and the Soviet successor states, but there is little coordination of effort. Greater collaboration or information exchange could avoid duplication and enhance the overall impact of foundation efforts.

Better coordination of humanitarian assistance and more energetic initiatives to dampen health risks should also be contemplated. The collapse of the health care system in Russia and Ukraine has produced an urgent need for better medical care. In addition, dangerous Chernobyl-type nuclear power plants continue to operate, posing substantial risk to human health far beyond Russian borders. A further German-American initiative could prod western nations to consider whether they should assume the primary burden of replacing these plants.

There are many possibilities. Some involve costs that may be unpopular at home. The question is whether both governments will take advantage of the opportunity offered by the German-American strategic fit to shape broader approaches to the east and sell the need for such initiatives to their citizens, or whether each will go its own way, picking its own preferences, perhaps loosely coordinating its efforts but generally refusing to assign priority to a more ambitious and better coordinated effort.

There is another, darker reason behind such a partnership. If democracy and economic stability are not established in Russia or Ukraine, there is potential for German-American acrimony. Germany's proximity and fear of destabilizing spillovers would give it relatively more incentive to focus on ways to stabilize the situation than the United States, which is more distant, generally more inclined to insist on certain standards of national behavior, and more willing to wield an array of political, economic and even military instruments on behalf of its position.

The Challenge of Ukraine

Ukraine poses an early test of such a partnership. A democratic, prosperous and secure Ukraine is crucial to stability, democratization, economic progress and arms control efforts throughout the former Soviet Union. It is a geostrategic buffer between Russia and central Europe.

If Ukraine remains independent, it is unlikely that Russia will again become an empire. But economic disaster looms. Inflation is raging, the currency has collapsed and the budget deficit is out of control. Chaos within is likely to be exploited from without. Ukraine has yet to undertake the kind of economic and political reforms needed to revive the economy and attract western investment. Many Russians still view Ukraine as a conditional entity. Should Ukraine implode and spur Russian intervention, Russian reform would be grievously harmed. Polish and Hungarian maneuvering room would be constrained. The coming year is crucial.

Fundamentally, the test is political. Neither the U.S. nor Germany has been sufficiently engaged to make a difference in Russian or Ukrainian behavior. They have not conveyed to the Russians their depth of feeling about Ukraine as a separate entity. Nor have they faced up to the contradictions in their own policies. If they are not prepared to give Ukraine necessary security guarantees or fold it into western economic structures, then they must face up to the fact that Ukraine almost certainly will be driven back into some form of association with Russia.

A German-American partnership could make a difference. A number of the initiatives proposed for Russia apply to Ukraine. The U.S. can also provide assistance on the safety, security and dismantling of nuclear weapons and compensate Ukraine for the sale of highly enriched uranium from former Soviet nuclear warheads. Germany could join the U.S. effort to construct an architecture of agreements and charters that reiterate joint support for Ukrainian independence. The U.S.-Ukrainian senior level strategic dialogue, which brings interagency teams on both sides to search for areas of cooperation, could be expanded to include Germany. Germany can also help with

THE WEST'S MILITARY INSTITUTIONS ARE FULL OF COLD WAR COBWEBS. THEY CANNOT SIMPLY BE GIVEN A GOOD DUSTING. THEY MUST BE REMADE.

confidence building mechanisms. Ukraine has received a draft text of security assurances from all five permanent members of the U.N. Security Council. Germany should echo those assurances.

Germany, fearing a deluge of 2 million ethnic German immigrants from the former Soviet Union, is working hard with Ukraine to create a viable homeland for them in a fertile area of southern Ukraine. With U.S. and broader western help, these aid efforts could be expanded to include non-ethnic Germans to blunt charges that the west is favoring specific groups within Ukraine. Again there are many possibilities. The question is one of political priority.

Remaking Collective Defense and Security

The West's military institutions are full of Cold War cobwebs. The waning light of old challenges and the sudden glare of new ones have cast shadows over current arrangements for collective defense and security. They cannot simply be given a good dusting. They must be remade.

NATO, the Conference on Security and Cooperation in Europe (CSCE) and the European Union as currently structured, the American troop presence as currently designed and American expenditures for "security" in Europe as currently distributed are mismatched with these new challenges. They not only require revamped security institutions, they demand a new relationship among them. NATO-or-nothing is no longer enough.

Here again Germany and America can be motors of change. We should work with the German government and the German Secretary General of NATO, Manfred Wörner, to build a new NATO and through it a new security relationship with the European Union. We should also work with the German Secretary General of the CSCE, Wilhelm Hoeynck, and the leaders of other European nations to make the CSCE more relevant to Europe's security challenges rather than try to stunt its growth out of misguided fear that it might compete with NATO.

A New NATO

NATO is down but not out. While the Soviet threat that defined much of NATO's rationale has disappeared, the alliance has developed other functions over the years that remain relevant: It assuages European fears about the potential uses of German power, promotes denation-

NATO'S PARTNERSHIP FOR PEACE CAN ONLY BE A STATION ALONG THE WAY TO A FUNDAMENTALLY NEW MILITARY RELATIONSHIP BETWEEN EAST AND WEST THAT WILL REQUIRE THE UNITED STATES TO CLARIFY WHETHER THE CONSOLIDATION OF DEMOCRACY IN THE REGION IS OF SUFFICIENT NATIONAL INTEREST TO EXTEND A SECURITY GUARANTEE.

alized military planning, forms a security foundation for efforts at European integration, provides the basis for joint multilateral actions and is the primary expression of America's commitment to Europe. Moreover, NATO is important to Germany. It gives many Germans a sense of stability and security in a time of bewildering change; it also allows Germany to continue to reject the possession or control of nuclear weapons for itself while retaining a voice on nuclear matters it would not otherwise have.

NATO's core purpose of collective defense must be maintained. To it must now be added the purposes of collective crisis management, force projection "out of area" and export of stability to the east. Given Europe's new security challenges, NATO will be unable to guarantee security in the west unless it is able to operate with non-NATO members in the east.

Precipitous enlargement of NATO, however, could undermine rather than enhance prospects for greater peace and stability in Europe. The practical reality is that east European nations are not ready to become NATO members overnight. Moving NATO suddenly to the Russian border could easily be misunderstood: It could create a Russian threat where there is not one today.

NATO's offer of a "partnership for peace" is a pragmatic effort to navigate these shoals. The proposal envisions a series of bilateral association agreements as codicils to the North Atlantic Treaty through which states would adhere to articles 1–4 of the treaty but not to the key mutual defense obligations contained in articles 5 and 6. The military relationships envisioned in the partnership for peace can support democratic institution-building by ensuring that peace partners civilianize their defense ministry, open their military budgets, develop habits of cooperation with NATO members and take the many necessary steps to ensure that the military functions productively within a civil society. The path toward collective self-defense obligations and military integration would denationalize defense policies and take concerns about each other out of the security risk calculations of member states.

Because NATO will not make any prima facie differentiation between possible partners, peace partners will begin to differentiate themselves as they work with NATO. Some may build links with NATO that could lead to full membership; others may exclude themselves

A NEW GERMAN-AMERICAN INITIATIVE COULD PROPOSE THAT NACC ADD NEUTRAL AND NON-ALIGNED MEMBERS PREVIOUSLY EXCLUDED FROM THE ORGANIZATION AND PROVIDE A FRAMEWORK OF COOPERATION FOR FLEXIBLE COALITIONS OF WILLING NATO AND NON-NATO MEMBERS.

from deeper defense collaboration by their failure to uphold principles enshrined in the North Atlantic Treaty, the Helsinki Final Act and the CSCE Charter of Paris.

There has been criticism that this proposal does not go far enough. But skeptics should not underestimate what is being offered. If peace partners take NATO's offer seriously, the potential to draw oneself closer within NATO's sphere of operations is high.

There are problems. First, this self-selecting process could breed the type of competition among east European nations that NATO seeks to avoid. Second, those who join the European Union are likely to be invited to join the West European Union (WEU). This will increase pressure to admit them to NATO as well. And even though NATO is reluctant to draw any new lines, at some point lines will have to be drawn as those peace partners that can meet NATO's criteria step up and announce their readiness.

Partnership for Peace can thus be only a station along the way to a fundamentally new military relationship between east and west that will require the United States to clarify whether the consolidation of democracy in the region is of sufficient national interest to extend a security guarantee.

Since this has not been the subject of national debate, the United States should avoid any process that makes full NATO membership automatic. Fulfilling the criteria is a necessary but not a sufficient condition for full membership. At that point NATO members should reserve the right to decide whether a commitment to mutual defense under Article 5 of the treaty is in their strategic interest.

It may well be in the U.S. national interest to commit men and women from Montana, Wisconsin and Virginia to defend the eastern borders of Poland, Slovenia and Hungary—but not without a major national debate. Such a commitment would be hollow if not rooted in firm domestic support. And such support is unlikely to come unless the administration launches a high-profile national campaign that underscores the relevance of a new NATO to U.S. national interests.

A second element in a new NATO is to develop the alliance's capabilities for crisis management, peacekeeping and peacemaking. These new roles demand a new relationship to the United Nations and the CSCE. Engaging in such operations at U.N. or CSCE request will lend greater international legitimacy to alliance efforts to dampen crises in the triangle of tension. This raises a new role for the North Atlantic Cooperation Council (NACC), which was formed at German-American initiative to help reconcile east and west after the collapse of communism. This original purpose has been transcended by NATO's partnership of peace proposal. A new German-American initiative could propose that NACC add neutral and non-aligned members previously excluded from the organization and provide a framework of cooperation for flexible coalitions of willing NATO and non-NATO members on such issues as peacekeeping operations, arms control agreements, antiproliferation and defense conversion.

Putting CSCE to Work

One important way the German-American strategic partnership could further invigorate multilateral mechanisms in this area would be to revitalize the CSCE by giving it more operational capabilities.

NATO is not designed to handle the problem of ethnic conflict. Yet that is arguably Europe's most pressing security threat The CSCE is much more active in trying to mediate these disputes, but it has little operational capability. The political and military aspects of conflict-prevention can come together if CSCE members are able to make more active use of the High Commissioner on National Minorities, their Forum for Security Cooperation and measures of collective preventive diplomacy such as early warning indicators. Such efforts should also include the dispatch of peacekeeping forces—under CSCE, U.N., NATO, NACC or even WEU aegis, whatever is most acceptable in the specific situation. There is no way to guarantee peaceful resolution of bitter European quarrels. But the knowledge that minorities can appeal to a recognized international authority can ease some tensions some of the time. So can assurances that groups determined to secede from a parent state have a peaceful means of getting a fair hearing. So could policies and procedures that underpin a people's "right to stay" in their home country rather than being forced by war or persecution to exercise their "right to leave." Equipping ourselves with flexible means to deal with instability is worth the effort. A German-American initiative in advance of the fall 1994 CSCE Review Meeting in Budapest could generate momentum.

Such an initiative should also acknowledge CSCE's limitations. None of the CSCE agreements has the force of treaty; they are inter-

BY THE END OF THE CENTURY NATO COULD IN EFFECT BECOME A BILATERAL U.S.-EU ALLIANCE.

governmental agreements. While the CSCE has diluted somewhat its unanimity principle, with more than fifty highly diverse members it is too unwieldy to serve as a collective defense organization. It has no experience in collective threat assessment or deterrent action. At the margin it can serve the cause of European security, but not at the expense of a weaker NATO or a diminished WEU. "If the alliance and/or the EC were to erode seriously in the 1990s," Robert Blackwill reminds us, "the CSCE would not be an inheritor of their mantles, but a parallel victim of their decline."

Flexible Defense

Third, the alliance must be rebalanced so that Europe assumes a fair share of responsibility. This means that the United States must be willing to allow Europeans to deal with crises on their doorstep should the United States be unwilling or unable. The U.S. should support efforts by its European allies to shift their forces away from territorial defense toward projection forces that can protect common vital interests outside the traditional NATO area. It should use these efforts to enshrine a new premise of collective defense: The United States should not be the only NATO member that can protect vital common interests outside of Europe. If the alliance was again forced to act in the Middle East and Western Europe had the ability just to double the two division contribution it made during the Gulf war, it could save the United States considerable blood and treasure.

In this regard NATO's second new initiative—combined joint task forces—is another pragmatic step forward. It is based on the notion that Europe's emerging defense identity should be separable but not separate from NATO. At every NATO subcommand a combined joint task force or planning cell will be established that conducts contingency planning for operations drawing on NATO assets but not involving all NATO members. NATO will still have the right of first refusal to deal with crises that do not automatically invoke Article 5 of the North Atlantic Treaty, but if it chooses not to take the lead it can turn to subgroups of the alliance such as the WEU. This would allow the WEU to use NATO infrastructure, command and control and logistics.

This adds needed flexibility to common defense efforts. To the extent the WEU or the Eurocorps use their new flexibility to bolster

Europe's force projection capabilities for out-of-area contingencies, they should receive a ringing American endorsement.

This effort is also a salutory attempt to square the circle of Franco-American differences within the alliance. Paris objects to what it sees as Washington's de facto veto over independent European military activities. Washington objects to slipping into new security commitments it opposes because of independent European initiatives. NATO's new flexibility could draw France back into closer defense cooperation with its NATO partners. France will never go back to old NATO, but it could join a new NATO. Even this possibility is unlikely under the present *cohabitation* arrangements. But behind the scenes there is movement. France is to start sending its defense minister to selected NATO meetings. The time before the French presidential elections should be used for quiet German-American initiatives to prepare the ground for full and active French participation.

A serious independent European military capability will be very slow in coming—if it comes at all. Efforts at common EU foreign and security policies will occupy the Europeans at least through the remainder of this decade. The need for U.S. strategic intelligence, lift and other assets to embark on any large-scale military action out of area, combined with Europe's general reluctance to go out on a limb without the United States, will give Washington opportunity for influence. But if Washington is to accept the combined joint task force idea, it must accept the full logic of the plan and abandon its traditional opposition to rapid and real European defense cooperation. If a robust European defense identity and military capability can be achieved, America should support it.

Furthermore, if the WEU eventually merges with the European Union, the United States would have equipped itself with a direct security link to the European Union via NATO—another much-needed dialogue mechanism. By the end of the century NATO could in effect become a bilateral U.S.-EU alliance.

Efforts at peacekeeping and force projection will work only if the alliance's resolve to prevent conflict is credible and accompanied by firm action. There are some worrying trends in this regard. For any alliance to be effective, member nations must continue to maintain a significant level of well-trained and well-equipped armed forces. Yet European defense budgets are in free fall. America's

HITLER'S CRIMES CONFER A PARTICULAR RESPONSIBILITY UPON A DEMOCRATIC GERMANY TO INVOLVE ITSELF FULLY AND FORTHRIGHTLY IN COLLECTIVE EFFORTS TO COMBAT GENOCIDAL-TYPE POLICIES THAT EVOKE NAZI EVILS. SUCH EFFORTS SHOULD NEVER BE LIMITED TO, BUT MUST INCLUDE, THE CREDIBLE WILL TO USE FORCE.

European partners are depriving themselves of any meaningful military capabilities for many years ahead. The alliance's array of forces determines its number of options. Just when a wider number of risks demands a wider number of options, NATO's choices are being narrowed.

Promoting German Strategic Maturity

The effectiveness of both a German-American strategic partnership toward the east and remade collective security structures hinge on the success of efforts to promote German strategic maturity.

What appears to be an overlap of interests between Germany and America in maintaining a close security relationship and keeping the U.S. involved in Europe hides important differences. These center on a decisive and divisive issue in German politics: whether the use of force is justified to defend the human rights and fundamental freedoms of other people faced with aggression.

This issue reveals highly divergent views regarding the purposes of collective defense and exposes the vacuum in strategic thinking that existed in Germany during the Cold War.

For many Germans, NATO and the U.S. military presence were seen as vehicles to defend Germany from a specific threat. They existed primarily to protect Germany. There was little concomitant understanding of NATO as a broader security alliance, as was evident in German waffling over support for Turkey in the Gulf war. The notion of being an "importer" of security has been ingrained in German attitudes for more than four decades. German reluctance even to discuss the possibility that Germany might have to use its power, including force, to protect others far from German soil is understandable given German history. It is a mindset that the Bonn Republic's allies encouraged and reinforced. The German political foundations have played an important role in democracy-building efforts abroad, but by and large a positive national tradition of Germany's exporting security to its allies, or protecting weaker nations from foreign aggression, is weak.

This way of thinking is proving insufficient to the realities of post-Soviet Europe. It does not allow the Germans to reflect naturally about the responsibilities that accompany the Berlin Republic's enhanced weight. It hinders the Germans from fulfilling their commitments within collective security organizations. It blocks the Germans from dealing effectively with crises within the triangle of tension on its doorstep. It encourages the tendency to argue for a narrow division of labor under which Germany concentrates on nonmilitary missions and nourishes a myopic moralism that rises to blister allies whenever they must confront grey challenges in the real world.

Moreover, it does not provide a sustainable base of popular support for an American troop presence. American taxpayers will support a substantial U.S. military presence in Germany only if it is seen to be a cost-effective investment in defending U.S. interests not just within NATO but beyond, which is where Europe's real security challenges lie. But if German voters do not share this rationale and do not accept that the use of force may at times be necessary in the face of aggression or gross violations of human rights, U.S. troops are too easily seen simply as a forward base of American power projection to pursue interests and policies that Germans do not necessarily share or support.

This special path relieves Germans from thinking more precisely about their national interests and values and what they must do to defend them if necessary. It means that allies won't know whether they can count on Germany in a crisis.

Can Germany Participate?

Time is running out on the meandering debate about full participation by German forces in collective security efforts outside the NATO area. None of the objections are persuasive. Foremost is the German constitution, which could be revised to allow German military missions out of area. The constitutional provisions in this regard are in fact vague, and one can argue about them in good faith.

But Germany's political class has allowed the debate to drag on so long that it threatens to undercut Germany's commitments to collective security. This is the message of none other than the German supreme court. The court's decision allowing German airmen to join AWACS missions over Bosnia was interesting not only for its result but also for its reasoning. If German airmen did not participate fully in such missions, the court argued, Bonn would forfeit its reputation as a reliable partner and would violate its alliance commitments. In other words, employing the *Bundeswehr* in service to the U.N. or NATO is a political choice, not a legal one. If Germany's political leaders want to amend the constitution, fine. But if Germany is to fulfill its responsibilities, it needs to change its ways of thinking, not its constitution.

The legacy of the Nazi war in the Balkans inhibits direct German military involvement in the area. Such reluctance is understandable, but does it mean that German troops should not participate in any collective defense of European territories once attacked by Nazi forces? For all practical purposes, this only leaves Sweden and Northern Ireland. The consequence of such an argument is to exclude—and excuse—Germany from any military contributions to collective efforts in turbulent areas in Eurasia. This turns the lessons of history on their head. Hitler's crimes confer a particular responsibility upon a democratic Germany to involve itself fully and forthrightly in collective efforts to combat genocidal-type policies that evoke Nazi evils. Such efforts should never be limited to, but must include, the credible will to use force.

To their credit, Chancellor Kohl and Defense Minister Volker Rühe are trying to coax their country along. German soldiers have been active in U.N. efforts in Cambodia, Somalia, Iraq and along the edge of Bosnia. But these activities are not yet grounded in a domestic consensus. The issue cuts across the political parties rather than between them, making resolution difficult.

Ironically, failure to come to grips with this issue is most likely to resonate within Germany itself: more refugee flows, greater exposure as a staging area for arms dealers and terrorists and a critically weakened alliance framework. Should NATO fade and Germany's eastern flank deteriorate, the Berlin Republic may face the very renationalization of German security and singularization of its position that for decades the Bonn Republic sought to avoid.

It is vital that the United States encourage Germany to develop the political and operational tools that would allow it to shift from being an importer of security to becoming an exporter of democratic stability. This will require a better understanding of the different perspectives each brings to the debate.

The United States can see Germany through its defense conundrums and help to shape the outlook of Germany's small but growing strategic community. A close working relationship is essential to American efforts to nudge Germany toward greater global responsi-

bilities in ways congruent to American interests. At the same time, a
heavy-handed American approach would only fuel the perception in
Germany that external pressures to assume greater global responsibilities simply reflect American desires rather than the consequences of Germany's enhanced weight. American leaders must
take great care to avoid the impression that they are forcing the
German domestic debate about greater global responsibility toward
specific American rather than German or broader western ends. The
debate must not be reduced to a narrow and insensitive focus on
the German use of force, which will handicap the more important
discussion of constructive channels for German power and the implications of Germany's new weight. The tone of the discussion will
be important. Sensitivities run high and the potential for misunderstanding is great.

The Bundeswehr: A Partial Partner?

If Germany positions itself politically and conceptually to adopt a
broader strategic perspective, it must also equip itself with relevant
capabilities.

Integrated military units are the cornerstone of a new-look NATO.
NATO's shrinking ground forces in Germany have been recast into
five army corps, all multinational, including a highly mobile rapid reaction corps under British command to deal with threats on Europe's
periphery and the Franco-German-Spanish-Belgian Eurocorps. U.S.
ground troops are being split into a pair of U.S.-German army corps,
one commanded by a German general and the other by an
American general.

U.S. forces have never been so tightly integrated with those of an
ally. For the first time an American division is being committed per-
manently to foreign commanders. It is a symbolic triumph for the
German-American partnership. But that triumph could look increasingly empty if the two corps remain simply political instruments to
provide cover for the need to maintain the German-American military
relationship. The German-American corps has no real military func-
tion as long as Germany is constrained from participating in out-of-
area contingencies. The *Bundeswehr* partner units are superbly
trained to deal with a threat that no longer exists, yet have neither the
training nor the readiness to deal effectively with new and more rele-

THE U.S. SHOULD REJECT GERMAN ATTEMPTS TO CREATE A DIVISION OF LABOR THAT ESSENTIALLY GIVES GERMANY A FREE HAND POLITICALLY AND ECONOMICALLY IN EASTERN EUROPE WHILE THE U.S. MILITARY COVERS ITS FLANKS ELSEWHERE.

vant contingencies. The American units in the two corps are among the most modern and well equipped in the United States military. The *Bundeswehr*'s most effective units have been assigned elsewhere— to NATO's reaction forces and the Eurocorps. And rather than creating new capabilities or even sustaining its old capabilities, the *Bundeswehr* is shrinking fast. It faces further drastic budget cuts of up to DM 2.4 billion.

Despite these problems, the *Bundeswehr* is determined to have a crisis reaction force in place and ready by the year 2000. The United States and other NATO allies can help, but it could be a perilous journey. Skeptics rightly ask what conceivable purpose these corps serve if German and American forces cannot fight shoulder to shoulder in common cause. At the moment they simply tie American soldiers to a German political class ridden by self-doubt.

Multinational units can simplify German participation in U.N. humanitarian or peacekeeeping operations and be an added source of legitimation for German participation in out-of-area operations. But they cannot substitute for the type of legitimacy that is rooted in a process within Germany that carefully considers such operations, determines they are important to German national interests, and then builds a national consensus to support them .

Such a process also carries consequences for America. If we encourage this new Germany, we must be prepared to give it a higher profile role in political and strategic decisionmaking. It means accepting the fact that Germany would frequently come to the table with its own strategic interests and perspectives. This will require a change in the way we conduct our business.

It also means accepting the fact that if the Berlin Republic is expected to participate in future multilateral out-of-area operations, it must create a modest national command structure to plan for such eventualities. Such a group is not the harbinger of a new German General Staff structure. Such a structure is neither appropriate nor necessary. But a smaller effort will allow German authorities to ground their participation in multinational activities in a firm appreciation of their value for Germany.

Some critics charge that the United States should seek exactly the opposite of what is proposed here. Instead of encouraging Germany, they argue we should contain it. They argue that it is a good thing

IF GERMANY'S POLITICAL LEADERS WANT TO AMEND THE CONSTITUTION, FINE. BUT IF GERMANY IS TO FULFILL ITS RESPONSIBILITIES, IT NEEDS TO CHANGE ITS WAYS OF THINKING, NOT ITS CONSTITUTION.

that the *Bundeswehr* has one foot tied to the stake. It is not. A containment policy would unleash resentment within Germany and unravel the alliance. It would damage other core American political and economic goals that are premised on a strong relationship with Germany. It would leave Washington ill-equipped to deal with turbulence in Russia and elsewhere in Eurasia. A stronger German capacity to act enhances both America's own ability to act when appropriate to U.S. interests and its flexibility to let Europeans cope with contingencies that do not warrant U.S. involvement. It also provides an essential justification for the continuation of an American troop presence in Germany.

Such an approach means rejecting German attempts, however well-meaning, to create a division of labor that essentially gives Germany a free hand politically and economically in eastern Europe while the U.S. military covers Germany's flanks elsewhere. A strategic partnership with Germany toward the east would convince Germans that the United States understands the nature of Europe's new security challenges and assigns high priority to a partnership with Germany that can cope with them. But the other half of the story is a German commitment to establish the political, conceptual and operational preconditions to fulfill its part of a new security bargain.

The U.S., Germany and the U.N.

Such a commitment is also a sine qua non of German membership in the United Nations Security Council. The international community cannot forego the credible threat and use of military force to maintain international law and protect human rights from gross violations. If Germany wants to be a permanent member of the Security Council, it cannot abstain from such efforts. German participation in Security Council activities, and NATO's ability to enforce Security Council resolutions in Europe will require a German military freed from its constitutional straitjacket but integrated into effective multilateral units trained and equipped to deal with crisis management and peacekeeping activities.

Here again U.S. support can be crucial and also advance U.S. interests. One simple and positive way to encourage broader German and Japanese strategic perspectives in anticipation of permanent Security Council membership is for the U.S. ambassadors in Bonn and Tokyo to be included in all relevant cable traffic involving the permanent members and then consult on a regular basis with German and Japanese officials on the issues involved. We should not create unrealistic expectations in Germany about our ability to change the membership of the Security Council. It will be difficult and take time. But taking the initiative to include German decisionmakers in issues affecting the permanent members of the Security Council will begin to build the habits of coordination and breadth of perspective necessary for effective German participation.

Redefining Transatlantic Economic Relations

A new security bargain is important. But it is only part of the story. More than ever, national security rests on economic strength. If Germans and Americans are prepared to update their security relations, they must be ready to reinvent transatlantic economic ties as well. If they do not, they risk undermining the alliance both are eager to maintain.

A new strategic bargain between Germany-in-Europe and America must take account of a change that is as revolutionary as the end of the Cold War: the radical and relentless makeover of the world economy, sparked by the globalization, automation and customization of manufacturing; the liberalization of capital flows and financial markets; the arrival of tough new competitors; the huge growth in service trade; and exceptional advances in information, technology and transportation. These changes are as unprecedented in their range and speed as they are uncertain in their ultimate consequences. They render traditional assumptions about trade, investment and monetary policies obsolete. They demand new terms of engagement between the world's leading economies.

The defining economic frame of the Cold War—American predominance in the global competition between capitalism and socialism—is gone. It has been transcended by a more ambiguous mixture of competition and cooperation between different forms of democratic capitalism. This has occurred at a time when Cold War constraints on economic conflict among allies have loosened and the United States is both more susceptible to global economic forces and less able to influence them unilaterally.

For the first time in sixty years the transatlantic relationship is being defined and tested as severely by economic as by security challenges. Global economic forces now impinge more directly and powerfully on the well-being of the average American or European than do military security issues. Unless more effective mechanisms can be developed to preempt and resolve economic and monetary conflicts between the advanced industrialized nations, the front lines of the post–Cold War era may be drawn between the victors of the Cold War themselves.

Fortunately, this is a time of opportunity. Transatlantic economic relations are at a watershed. A recent series of milestone events—the successful completion of the Uruguay Round of multilateral trade negotiations, the birth of the North American Free Trade Agreement (NAFTA), the transformation of the old European Community into a deeper and wider European Union, the creation of the European Economic Area (EEA), and efforts to strengthen the nascent Asian-Pacific Economic Cooperation forum (APEC)—mark a new global economic era. The United States and Germany should build on these successes by working with their partners to craft a new transatlantic economic strategy that relates immediate, doable policy goals to a broader vision.

Pacific Promises, Atlantic Realities[1]

Unfortunately, Europe has become unfashionable to Americans focused on events at home and across the Pacific. The promise of the Pacific is great, but we ignore Europe at our peril.

By any measure, the nations of the European Union rank among our premier economic partners. It is true that the importance of

---

Chart 4

**Market Shares
for U.S. Trade**

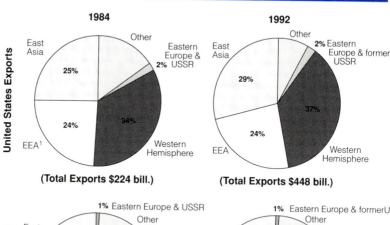

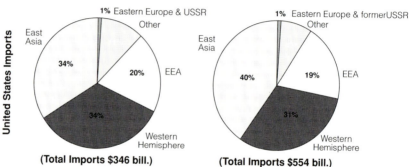

[1] EEA: The European Economic Area comprises the 12 nations of the European Union and five members of the European Free Trade Association.
Source: *1993 Direction of World Trade Statistics Yearbook, 1992 Direction of World Trade Statistics Yearbook*

transatlantic trade is diminishing both in the bilateral context and for the world economy as a whole. U.S. trade is shifting to Asia. So is Europe's, even though the volume of transatlantic trade has increased steadily. America's transpacific trade of $316 billion in 1992 was about one and a half times larger than the $221 billion with Western Europe, but two-thirds of the transpacific total represents imports from Asia, mostly from Japan. This imbalance creates more friction than jobs, even though it benefits American consumers. Exports across the Pacific and Atlantic are more evenly balanced: The U.S. exports $128 billion in goods and services annually to APEC countries and $102 billion to Europe. And the United States has a small trade surplus with Europe, compared with an $89 billion deficit with East Asia.

Moreover, single-minded attention to trade ignores investment flows, which in the new global economy may prove to be more consequential for jobs and productivity, and which are dominated by ·

Chart 5

**Market Shares
for German Trade**

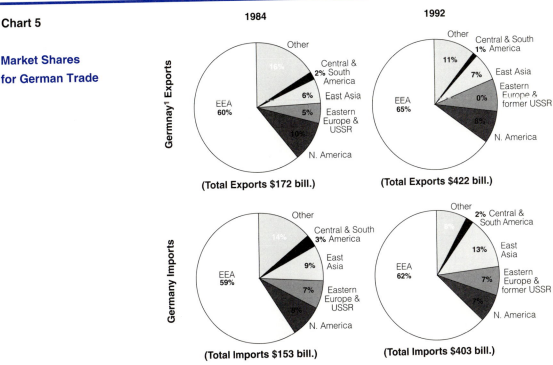

1 1984-western Germany; 1992-united Germany

Source: *1993 Direction of World Trade Statistics Yearbook, 1992 Direction of World Trade Statistics Yearbook*

Europe and America. During the past decade foreign investment has grown three times faster than world trade and four times faster than world output. In the new global economy foreign investment drives trade and is the primary engine of growth. Investment flows across the Atlantic continue to rise dramatically, dwarfing transpacific flows. Investment stocks are similarly skewed toward Europe. U.S. investments in Europe through 1992 totaled $239 billion—eclipsing American investment in the rest of the world. EC investments in the United States totaled $249 billion—again more than half of Europe's overall global investments. Intra-company trade now accounts for half of total transatlantic trade. Forty-nine percent of U.S. foreign investment abroad is in Europe; only 16 percent is in Asia. U.S. investments in Asia amounted to only $78 billion; Asian investments in the U.S. totalled $108 billion. And while Asia will become more important as a source of investment in the United States, during the past four years its share of total U.S. foreign direct investment abroad rose only by 1 percent.

European firms provide more jobs in the U.S. than do the affiliates of all other nations combined. Exports to Europe support 4.2 million American jobs. More than 4,000 European-owned firms in the U.S. provide jobs in every state and directly employ an additional 3 million American workers. European firms directly account for 7 percent of U.S. manufacturing employment.

When indirect employment fueled by European-owned firms' demands for raw materials, capital and other inputs is considered, the

Graph 1

U.S. Trade Balance with EU and Germany

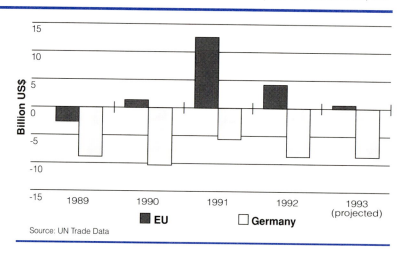

Source: UN Trade Data

total employment figure from exports to Europe and European investment in the U.S. jumps to 11.9 million jobs, or 11.1 percent of all U.S. private sector employment. And European firms do not just create jobs, they create high-skill, high-wage jobs. Half of those European-supported American jobs and one-third of European investment is concentrated in the high-wage, high-tech manufacturing sector. European subsidiaries pay wages 20 percent higher on average than those of American firms. They funnel hundreds of billions of dollars into the economy in the form of payroll, capital, operating and research and development expenditures. Even in California, a state where Asian economic ties are highly visible, more investment comes from Europe than from Japan; 43 percent of the $77.5 billion invested in California from around the world is from Europe.

In addition, western Europe increasingly speaks with one voice on international economic matters. The European Union, not Japan, held the key to unlocking the stalemate on world trade talks. And unlike Asia's mélange of nations, the European Union could inflict great harm on the United States in a trade war.

There is great potential in the emerging markets of Asia and Latin America. But it would be foolhardy to assign priority to regions of promise at the expense of weighty and proven economic ties. China's economic growth is certain to change the world. But at present the 17 million people of the German state of Northrhine-Westphalia export more than do the 1.4 billion people of China. The

Chart 6

**U.S. Direct Investment
Abroad
Percent Share 1991**

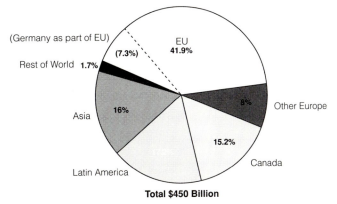

Source: OECD; Congressional Research Service

**MORE THAN EVER, NATIONAL
SECURITY RESTS ON
ECONOMIC STRENGTH. IF
GERMANS AND AMERICANS
ARE PREPARED TO UPDATE
THEIR SECURITY RELATIONS,
THEY MUST BE READY TO
REINVENT TRANSATLANTIC
ECONOMIC TIES AS WELL.**

gross domestic product of only two German states—Northrhine-Westphalia and Bavaria—tops the combined gross domestic product of Asia's "four tigers" of Singapore, Hong Kong, Taiwan and South Korea. And the 418 million people living in all of Central and South America produce less than do the 57 million people living in Italy.

The real headline is not that Europe or Asia is the more important economic partner, but that the economic health of each region has become absolutely critical to America's economic health. Economics is not a zero sum game. Americans do not lose when other peoples become more prosperous. Greater prosperity elsewhere means new markets for American business and new jobs for American workers. American consumers can choose among a broader spectrum of both lower cost and higher quality goods. Capital flows from abroad help finance our massive deficits. The United States has become as dependent as Japan or the EU as a whole on trade and foreign investment for its economic prosperity. Europe and Asia are vital to any hopes of sustained U.S. economic recovery.

In this context, our economic and monetary relations with Germany will be pivotal. Germany's prime economic importance to the United States remains its role as the principal financial and economic power within the European Union. A goal of singular importance to the U.S. is to support German efforts to champion open and competitive markets within the European Union, throughout Europe and around the world. Without vigorous U.S. efforts, such a German approach is by no means a foregone conclusion.

Germany is a major global economic power and the key economic force in Europe. It is both partner and competitor for the United States. Germany alone, with a population of 80 million, regularly vies with the U.S., with a population of 260 million, as the largest exporter in the world. The *Deutsche Mark*, not the yen, is the world's second reserve currency and the monetary anchor of Europe's single market. The United States is the single main source of foreign investment in Germany and the primary target of German foreign investment around the world. By the end of 1989 German direct investment in the United States accounted for 30 percent of total German direct investments abroad, and U.S.investments in Germany comprised 30 percent of all foreign direct investment in Germany. More than 2,400 German companies are active in the

United States, mainly in the chemical industry and in electrical engineering, with a payroll of almost 500,000 employees. American investments in Germany are also concentrated in manufacturing, primarily office and data processing equipment and autos, followed by holding companies and property administration. German investments expand America's economic base, create jobs, introduce new products and services using advanced technology, increase U.S. productivity and strengthen the balance of payments through capital inflows and the substitution of domestic goods and services for imports.

Although the two nations are robust economic competitors, a complementary pattern of exchange has evolved that enables companies in both nations to exploit different competitive advantages, particularly in high wage, high value-added manufacturing goods and industrial supplies. Both nations have developed competitive advantages that allow them to create profitable specialized markets in other highly industrialized information economies.

Both nations share important economic interests. Both want and need an open world system of trade and investment. Both would prefer predictable exchange rate relationships and harmonized interest rate policies. Both want to avoid competitive devaluations and pro-

Graph 2

U.S.-German Bilateral Direct Investment Position at Year-end

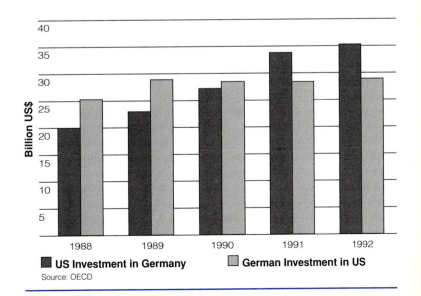

Source: OECD

tectionist measures that evoke memories of the hyperinflation of the 1920s in Germany or the Great Depression of the 1930s.

But direct economic competition is intensifying as banks and firms in both countries expand their exports, investments and financial activities. Such competition has already become quite intense in the dynamic economies of Asia, particularly China.

Moreover, real differences exist between German and American approaches to economic and monetary policies. The legislative mandates of both central banks are also quite different. Whereas American policies lean toward Keynesian concepts of demand management, Germans emphasize monetary stability, not only as a principal goal of policy but an important objective in its own right. America's accent on economic liberalism, marked by distant and often antagonistic relations between government, business and labor, contrasts with Germany's brand of corporative capitalism, which is characterized by a dense network of cooperative ties between government, industry and labor.

These differences often inflame the relationship. The United States regularly criticizes German monetary policies for being overly restrictive and thus constraining European and global growth. Not only do German officials usually resist such cajoling, they point to what they

Graph 3

Composition of German Exports

Over 85 percent of German exports are manufactures.

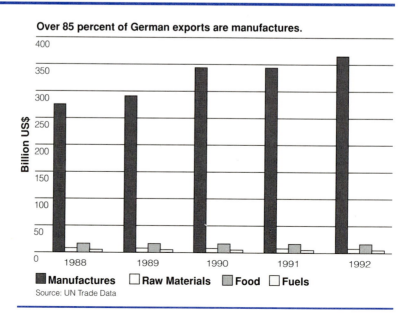

Source: UN Trade Data

see as sins of American fiscal and monetary policy. Given the growing interconnections between the two economies, this failure to agree
on appropriate priorities of fiscal and monetary policy could become
one of the most contentious aspects of the relationship.

Trade disputes could further exacerbate those difficulties.
Tensions with the EU over the Uruguay Round of multilateral trade
negotiations exposed a critical gap between U.S. expectations of
Germany's new role and expectations within Germany itself. The
continuing inability of the EU to agree to reforms for its Common
Agricultural Policy in the face of massive pressure from Washington
and other trading partners was a disturbing portent. While France
was a major force blocking change, Germany was central to
European obstinence—another important illustration that what
Germany does not do in the new age can be as important as what it
does. The ultimate compromise left a somewhat bitter taste.

On a range of issues essential to the international economy,
German and American views differ significantly. Managing these
differences requires constant attention. Without vigorous U.S. engagement, German and American expectations of the responsibilities incumbent upon themselves and their partners for the efficient
operation of the international economy could diverge in important
ways. Unless the United States helps Europe maintain an outward
focus, unless Europe continues to invest in America and import
U.S. products at a high rate, unless Europeans and Americans

Graph 4

**Composition
of German Exports
of Manufactured Goods**

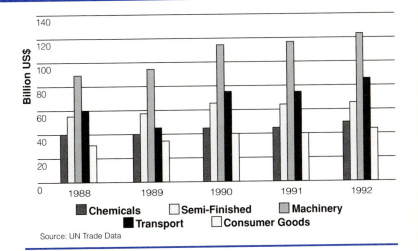

Source: UN Trade Data

work together to clear away new hurdles to trade and investment, unless there is transatlantic cooperation in monetary affairs, President Clinton's program of domestic economic renewal is unlikely to succeed.

Inordinate American preoccupation with Asia and domestic economic issues could leave U.S. leaders and the American public unprepared for the economic and financial challenges posed by the rapid changes underway in Europe, which could alter long-held assumptions that have guided the global economy. The dense network of relations created during the postwar period will cushion the impact of future misunderstandings and soften periodic clashes of interests and perspective, but if relations with Europe in general and Germany in particular are neglected or their significance underestimated by preoccupied political leaders, such disputes could become more frequent and contentious, tearing at the partnership.

Unless U.S. economic relations with Europe are infused with a new strategic vision, they will be hostage to circumstances. European-American divorce could come about more by default than by design.

Our interests compel us to engage actively in Europe. To advance those interests effectively in the new global economy we must—and now can—change the manner of our European engagement. Seven steps are required.

Graph 5

**Composition
of German Imports**

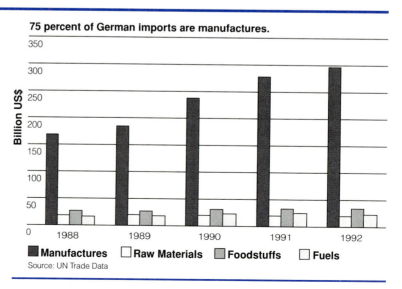

75 percent of German imports are manufactures.

Billion US$

■ **Manufactures** ☐ **Raw Materials** ▨ **Foodstuffs** ☐ **Fuels**

Source: UN Trade Data

Taking Europe Seriously

First, Washington must take European integration seriously. On November 1, 1993, the Maastricht Treaty gave birth to a European Union that is more than the European Community writ large. Maastricht gives the European Parliament the right of co-decision with the Council of Ministers on legislation affecting the huge internal market. It deepens collaboration between governments on drugs, immigration and crime, lays the groundwork for greater cooperation on foreign policy and sets the stage for a single European currency. The forerunner to a European Central Bank, the European Monetary Institute, was formally set up on January 1, 1994, and will open its doors in Frankfurt this year.

Maastricht builds on the Community's "1992" program of creating a single European market, which has dramatically changed the way Europeans do business. Capital, goods and people move more freely than ever between the Twelve. Layers of national regulation are being replaced by Union-wide directives. National industrial policies are giving way to Europe-wide policies that are generally more market-friendly. In areas such as financial services and government procurement the EU may be moving towards more comprehensive market liberalization than the United States and could make access to its own market contingent upon changes in U.S. laws and regulations. The extension of EU competence into new policy areas means that

Graph 6

**Composition
of German Imports of
Manufactured Goods**

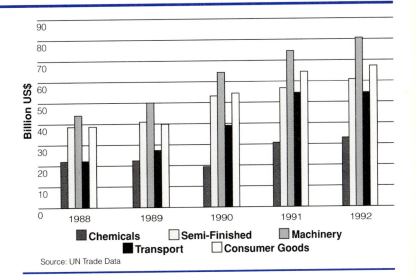

Source: UN Trade Data

EUROPEAN INTEGRATION HAS REACHED SUCH A SIGNIFICANT STAGE THAT NEW TRANSATLANTIC COMPONENTS MUST BE BUILT INTO A DEEPER AND WIDER EUROPEAN UNION.

the Union will become a more powerful and assertive bargaining partner for the U.S.

Moreover, the European Union is part of an even broader European Economic Area (EEA) comprising the EU and five wealthy members of the European Free Trade Association. Within the next few years the Union could take in some of Europe's wealthiest countries—Finland, Sweden, Norway, Austria—and some of its newest markets—the Czech and Slovak Republics, Hungary and Poland.

In short, the rather abstract question that continues to enthrall most commentators—whether the European Community will opt for "widening" over "deepening"—is yesterday's news. It has been superseded by the practical reality of a multi-speed Europe anchored to the German core. Rather than a tightly knit community marching in lock-step toward deeper unity that was envisioned by its founders, the European Union is quickly becoming what it has traditionally sought to avoid: a more fluidly defined democratic community of variable geometry, a mobile of different levels and forms of association, all moving fitfully and at different speeds toward closer forms of cooperation. As it spins, its final shape and nature are up for grabs.

Some aspects of European integration will challenge U.S. policies; others will provide new openings. All point to the need for a strengthened U.S. bilateral relationship with the EU and the need for the U.S. to define more clearly what it expects from Europe. The fluid nature of "Europe" offers Washington ample opportunities to influence developments in ways that advance American and broader global interests—*if* we understand the degree to which our economic future is linked to that of Europe, and *if* we ourselves know what kind of European Union we want.

The Need for Flexible Dialogue Mechanisms

America should not try to seat itself at the formal table of European Union. Such an effort would only arouse suspicion and be counterproductive. Washington should be also forthright about its support for deeper and wider European integration. But this support should be coupled with the expectation that European integration has reached such a significant stage that a variety of flexible dialogue mechanisms are now needed between the United States and the European

SINGLE-MINDED ATTENTION TO TRADE IGNORES INVESTMENT FLOWS, WHICH IN THE NEW GLOBAL ECONOMY MAY PROVE TO BE MORE CONSEQUENTIAL FOR JOBS AND PRODUCTIVITY, AND WHICH ARE DOMINATED BY EUROPE AND AMERICA.

Union to ensure that wider and deeper European integration strengthens, rather than weakens, transatlantic cooperation. EU-U.S. disputes become acrimonious in part because there is no political commitment to a process of shared strategic view that transcends disputes over such individual issues as taxation, antitrust, beef hormones or lawnmower regulations.

It is fashionable to question Europe's progress toward deeper union. But if one looks below the surface of European squalls, one can see quite clearly the force that is slowly but irrevocably binding Europe together: the daily process of mutual interaction between European societies and between their governments. Whether this leads to a common foreign policy or not, European decisionmakers consult, test, argue and eventually coordinate a range of policies on a daily basis. A large part of what European nations once considered the domain of foreign policy has become, in effect, European domestic policy. This daily dynamic is influencing the integration process in important ways but is usually overlooked by commentators transfixed by institutional arrangements.

American decisionmakers must be more actively engaged in this process. For instance, U.S. policy should give priority to efforts that invigorate regular channels of dialogue between German and other key European political directors and their policy-level counterparts in the State Department and other agencies. A range of possibilities come to mind that take advantage of the U.S. government's interactive Worldnet facilities. A monthly Worldnet dialogue between senior Environmental Protection Agency (EPA) officials, their counterparts at the German Ministry of the Environment and environmental officals from other European nations could be a productive start. A similar channel between U.S. Labor Department and German and European Labor Ministry officials on issues of learning and competitiveness, or between Health and Human Services and German and other European counterparts on health care issues could be useful. Other mechanisms are feasible. The point is to accord political priority to the process.

Coping with Regionalization

The second step is to ensure that the creation of NAFTA, a stronger APEC, and the European Economic Area serve to strengthen, rather

THE REAL HEADLINE IS NOT THAT EUROPE OR ASIA IS THE MORE IMPORTANT ECONOMIC PARTNER, BUT THAT THE ECONOMIC HEALTH OF EACH REGION HAS BECOME ABSOLUTELY CRITICAL TO AMERICA'S ECONOMIC HEALTH.

than weaken transatlantic and broader multilateral economic relations. The post–Uruguay Round world will be shaped by free trade agreements and freer trading areas. The three NAFTA economies consist of 370 million people, account for 18 percent of world trade, and generate output worth $6.8 trillion. The seventeen nations of the European Economic Area house 372 million people, generate a collective gross national product (GNP) of $7.5 trillion and account for 46 percent of world trade. The nations of APEC (including its three NAFTA members) account for over 2 billion people (more than half in China), account for 39 percent of world trade and have a combined gross domestic product of $14 trillion.

Neither NAFTA nor APEC is as ambitious as the European Union. NAFTA is a free trade union, not a customs union, and is certainly not the harbinger of North American political, economic and monetary union. Canada and Mexico have much smaller economies than the U.S.; they depend on it for almost three-quarters of their trade. All three are also members of APEC. APEC, created in 1989, is still in its infancy. It is a diverse collection of countries whose ambitions and abilities vary greatly. But members of APEC, both through NAFTA and at the November 1993 Seattle summit, have sent clear signals that they are determined to set an ambitious course of liberalization.

How collaboration proceeds within each region, and how these economic areas deal with each other, will be decisive for the global economy. Multilateral economic negotiations are likely to focus more and more on harmonizing the results of these different regional schemes.

Regionalization will affect the transatlantic relationship in important but as yet indeterminate ways. Regional accords can be healthy if they accelerate trade reforms and serve as building blocks for further multilateral liberalization in trade, investment and services. Razing economic walls within regions without raising them between regions is good for the world economy and compatible with GATT. A stronger European entity could be a stronger partner for the United States on a range of global issues.

But regionalization could create two inward-looking and less engaged entities, less interested in broader cooperation and less interested in one another. Unless concerted action is taken, regional economic experiments could contest rather than complement multi-

THE RATHER ABSTRACT QUESTION THAT CONTINUES TO ENTHRALL MOST COMMENTATORS—WHETHER THE EUROPEAN COMMUNITY WILL OPT FOR "WIDENING" OVER "DEEPENING"— IS YESTERDAY'S NEWS. IT HAS BEEN SUPERSEDED BY THE PRACTICAL REALITY OF A MULTI-SPEED EUROPE ANCHORED TO THE GERMAN CORE.

lateralism. Moreover, unilateral European or North American attempts to limit or restrict Asian access to their respective markets could richochet.

To preempt this possibility APEC and the European Economic Area should at a minimum create regular consultative mechanisms to deal with frictions that are bound to arise and make active use of GATT's much-improved dispute settlement mechanisms. APEC's curt brush-off of the European Union's request for observer status at the November 1993 APEC summit in Seattle should be reviewed.

Procedures for preventive economic diplomacy should also be devised between the EEA and APEC's sub-regional grouping of NAFTA. The economic growth and liberalization in Mexico resulting from NAFTA is likely to result in a sharp increase of trade with the European Economic Area and in more European investment, but NAFTA raises a host of issues for the Europeans in such areas as financial services, public procurement and agriculture. An EEA-NAFTA consultative mechanism might be able to clear away problems in these areas before they generate deeper tensions.

Seen in this way, regional arrangements can truly be building blocs for a reinvigorated multilateral system of trade and investment. As both an Atlantic and Pacific power, the United States is the pivot. It is the world's largest economy, a member of both APEC and NAFTA, and continues to underwrite Europe's security and hence its prosperity. Washington should take the initiative to launch such dispute-dampening mechanisms.

Widening Transatlantic Economic Relations

The third step in a new strategy is to develop a coherent U.S. approach to the coming enlargement of the European Union. The EU is committed in principle to doubling the number of its member states and adding 100 million people during the next ten years—a fundamental reorientation of the idea of Europe itself as defined during the Cold War. Enlargement raises a host of economic, political and security implications for the United States and could distract European attention from important transatlantic issues unless the United States finds a way to advance its interests in the process.

Throughout the Cold War the United States gave strong political support to expansion of the EC. The economic consequences for

**MULTILATERAL ECONOMIC
NEGOTIATIONS ARE LIKELY
TO FOCUS MORE AND MORE
ON HARMONIZING THE
RESULTS OF DIFFERENT
REGIONAL SCHEMES.**

the United States of such efforts, which in some cases were quite significant, were dismissed as secondary to the security benefits to the west of expanding the community of European democracies in the face of the Soviet threat. Without that threat, the security-economic hierarchy regarding enlargement is less clear. Membership in the European Union is probably the most important single step toward consolidating democracies and market economics in eastern Europe, but enlargement with no consideration of its consequences for the transatlantic economic relationship is a recipe for friction.

Problems are already apparent. Uncoordinated aid and trade initiatives undermine broader western efforts to consolidate democracies and market economies in the east. At the same time the G-24 was assembling a hefty aid package for eastern Europe and Russia, the EC and the U.S. imposed punitive duties and quantitative restrictions on "cheap" eastern imports. During negotiations to create a pan-European Energy Charter the EC rebuffed a U.S. proposal to apply the principle of "national treatment" to energy investments in favor of a Russian proposal to apply the more restrictive principle of reciprocity. Hungary froze economic negotiations with the United States because it was reluctant to agree to anything that might jeopardize its application for EC membership.

Perhaps the most daunting challenge is in agriculture, which has been a point of heated contention between the U.S. and the EC for decades and brought the Uruguay Round to the brink of failure. Once the EU incorporates into its Common Agricultural Policy regions that historically were the breadbasket of Europe, earlier tensions will seem minor in comparison with new agricultural clashes unless there is a transatlantic mechanism that anticipates and preempts them. A U.S.-EU agricultural working group on the issue of EU enlargment, for instance, might be appropriate, as would working groups on other sensitive sectors such as steel.

The German-American strategic partnership outlined in the previous chapter could generate useful initiatives that would allow both sides to prepare the ground together for enlargement, which in broader strategic perspective is clearly a shared transatlantic goal.

A EUROPEAN-AMERICAN INVESTMENT INITIATIVE WOULD TARGET THE AREA MOST LIKELY OVER THE NEXT FEW YEARS TO BENEFIT U.S. COMPANIES AND CREATE JOBS.

Deepening the Relationship: *A Transatlantic Investment Code*

The Cold War economic order was macro; the new economic order is micro. Domestic regulations and microeconomic policies loom as prominent barriers to international commercial activities now that significant tariff and non-tariff barriers have been stripped away by multilateral negotiations. A fourth step creating greater economic opportunities across the Atlantic is to explore bottom-up solutions that create groundrules of engagement in a range of microeconomic areas such as investment, competition, technology, regulations and standards and policies toward industry.

The centerpiece of such transatlantic microeconomic initiatives should be investment. Globalization of production is altering the relationship between trade and investment in fundamental ways. Whereas trade was often seen as leading the way for foreign investment, today the equation is being reversed. In more and more industries, from auto parts to steel, competitive success is based on customization and service, and these generally require a local presence in the foreign market. Moreover, the fact that rapid technological change makes it impossible to maintain a competitive edge based on technological prowess for anything but a brief interval means that the most successful companies are those that not only can introduce products quickly but simultaneously in domestic and foreign markets—another factor pushing foreign direct investment. In addition, recent studies have shown that foreign direct investment is far more powerful than trade as a force for improving productivity, particularly in Germany and the United States.

Foreign-owned companies in the U.S. and U.S. companies operating abroad both make significant contributions to the U.S. economy. The government does not need to choose between supporting a U.S. company abroad or a foreign company in the United States. Rather, it should seek to promote conditions at home and abroad that enable all companies to contribute to U.S. economic welfare.

Attracting foreign investment to the United States can also mean attracting export capacity. The new BMW plant in South Carolina and the planned Mercedes-Benz plant in Alabama will both produce vehicles that as yet do not exist for a market that does not yet exist. Both companies seek to use the United States as a base from which to

TRANSATLANTIC MECHANISMS ON MICROECONOMIC ISSUES COULD BLAZE TRAILS FOR MULTILATERAL EFFORTS TO DEFINE COMMON GROUNDRULES OF THE GLOBAL ECONOMIC GAME.

create new export markets. Two-thirds of the production will be exported abroad—a boost to the U.S. trade balance.

Foreign subsidiaries of U.S. companies also benefit the U.S. economy by penetrating foreign markets and expanding U.S. exports. Contrary to the assertions of critics, foreign affiliates generally do not produce goods for the U.S. market that might otherwise be made in the U.S. Excluding Canadian affiliates, 92 percent of manufacturing affiliate sales in 1989 went to non-U.S. markets—64 percent to the local market and 28 percent to third country markets. Only 8 percent of the sales of these foreign affiliates were in the U.S. market. U.S. direct investment abroad provides a platform for export growth and thus supports American jobs. The $200 billion in exports by U.S. manufacturing multinationals in 1990 accounted for 2.4 million U.S. jobs and resulted in a trade surplus of $80 billion. Foreign subsidiaries of U.S. companies generate earnings for reinvestment in the U.S. and are the single most positive factor in the U.S. balance of payments. Positive trade flows and earnings net of reinvestment from foreign affiliates hit $130 billion in 1990. Foreign subsidiaries also provide access to foreign technology not available in the U.S. Finally, U.S. investment abroad allows companies to integrate their worldwide operations and form strategic alliances which promote the competitiveness of the U.S. parent.

Investment has become the largest and fastest-growing aspect of the transatlantic relationship. But there is no investment regime that could spur such flows and limit abuses. The region from Honolulu to Hamburg has become a common investment area without common groundrules.

The growing importance of investment is already reshaping global economic negotiations. It also points to the growing importance of sub-national actors, particularly in the German-American economic relationship. States and regions within nations increasingly negotiate directly with multinational corporations to lure investments that create jobs and raise tax revenues. Sometimes such activities pit the interests of national governments against their own states and regions, as when Charlotte, North Carolina, was seeking to attract Lufthansa at the same time that U.S. negotiators were trying to strike a very different deal with German authorities on landing rights. Such activities raise the spectre of beggar-thy-neighbor bidding wars between states and regions within nations as well as between nations for scarce investment resources. Desperate regional competitors are resorting increasingly to bribery via subsidies or public infrastructure investments.

The tactics employed by Alabama in its ultimately successful bid to lure Mercedes-Benz are likely to be a precursor, rather than an exception, to the new era unless basic groundrules are established. The state offered more than $300 million in subsidies, gave multi-year tax exemption, and agreed to pay the salaries of 1,500 Mercedes workers during a year of training in exchange for an investment valued at only $350 million, at the same time that the state is under court order to spend more than $500 million a year upgrading its schools.

States use taxpayers' money to clinch such deals yet rarely provide a full accounting of total costs. And often there is no real increase in jobs but a shift in jobs from one state to another, even across the ocean. While companies play states off against one another, public coffers are drained. Such deals may even be a technical violation of the minimal GATT guidelines that do exist. In the absence of firmer common groundrules nations may undertake tit-for-tat retaliation by imposing discriminatory legislation on foreign investment or threatening market closure through anti-dumping duties, domestic content requirements and other forms of administered protection.

The sources of tension in the transatlantic investment agenda are fundamental, stemming in part from overlapping jurisdictions governing investment both in the U.S. and the EU, from increasing revenue requirements and concerns over employment on both sides of the Atlantic. European-based corporations worry about U.S. federal tax regulations, the outlook for unitary taxes such as those imposed by California and future U.S. policy toward inward investment. American companies worry about "forced" investment in some sectors and restricted investment opportunities in others.

German/European and American authorities should work vigorously to remove trade and investment barriers as they affect both foreign-owned companies in each other's markets and their own national companies operating abroad. There is a need to design a transatlantic investment regime that would tackle current problems and prevent new disputes from arising. A U.S.-EU foreign invest-

A BILATERAL INITIATIVE ON LEARNING AND COMPETITIVENESS CAN BUILD NEW COALITIONS ACROSS THE ATLANTIC. IT CAN STRENGTHEN THE BILATERAL RELATIONSHIP AT THE SAME TIME IT ADVANCES OUR ECONOMIC AND EDUCATIONAL GOALS.

ment code would be the best first step. The code would reaffirm non-discrimination of mutual investment based on the principle of "national treatment." If European and American firms were treated as national firms in each other's markets, many of the greatest obstacles to bilateral investment would never arise. The United States has bilateral investment agreements with individual European nations affirming the principle of national treatment, but there is no such agreement with the European Union. And the EU has shown signs of backing away from that principle. Other elements might include better coordinated antitrust and enforcement; more predictable tax treatment; and better coordinated technical and regulatory regimes. A clearer delineation of authority between federal and state governments would be particularly helpful in the German-American relationship, given the federal nature of each system. The code could lay out common rules for participation in government high-tech consortia so that arguments of "national security" do not become an excuse for protectionism. Finally, the code should contain an evolutionary clause that would allow the partners to build on what has been accomplished.

A European-American investment initiative would target the area most likely over the next few years to benefit U.S. companies and create jobs. During the past few years EU countries have been attracting $65–$70 billion annually in new outside investment, more than half from the U.S. The European single market has not only accelerated cross-European company alliances, but those with American firms as well. Moreover, European governments squeezed by budget deficits are beginning a massive sell-off of state companies, with as much as $150 billion at stake, creating enormous profit opportunities for U.S. foreign investors and investment banks—if the groundrules are clear.

Other Microeconomic Compacts

A transatlantic investment compact can be accompanied by similar agreements on a number of other microeconomic issues, such as domestic standards and regulations. Globalization of production has increased the commercial significance of differences in national rules of competition, business and regulatory policies. It has created a need for basic guidelines.

Incompatible standards, or the way countries certify that products comply with standards, have become major stumbling blocks to trade and investment. Germany's bureaucratic product standards, testing, labeling and certification regulations and procedures can prove a baffling maze. The EU is harmonizing differing national standards and testing and certification procedures into a single EU-wide body of uniform standards and regulations. It has developed a growing body of European law that is little understood within the United States yet significant for multinational companies operating in world markets. EU law is also likely to be the standard underpinning business relationships throughout eastern Europe and various Soviet successor states.

The different regulatory regimes vexing transatlantic economic relations are becoming sufficiently contested and complex to suggest the need to create a regular bilateral U.S.-EU consultative mechanism on standards to ensure that the interests of the partner are recognized in the evolution of U.S. and EU transnational laws, with the aim of writing regulations that are mutually compatible so as to preempt barriers down the road. Since German standards are generally high and exert influence on the standard-setting process throughout Europe, better U.S.-German coordination is important.

The 1991 U.S.-EC agreement on competition policy, for example, which has made bilateral collaboration more effective and systematic, could be extended and serve as a model for similar pacts with Japan and other advanced industrialized nations. Including the EU in the bilateral U.S.-Japanese Structural Impediments Initiative, to take another example, would mean that the standards agreed upon would be clearly international and would lend more weight to efforts to ensure that different forms of capitalism are compatible.

Learning and Competitiveness

The new information economy is human capital intensive. The rapid pace of change requires workers who are not only educated in depth—given highly specialized skills in their field to allow them to work in well-paid, highly productive jobs—but also educated in breadth to develop the knowledge, flexibility and ability to adapt to change so they are not left without a usable set of workplace skills should they need to switch jobs. Workers need to be educated not

THE ISSUE OF LEARNING AND COMPETITIVENESS IS NOT JUST ONE-WAY. MANY OF GERMANY'S DEFICIENCIES ARE AMERICA'S STRENGTHS.

only to get their first job but to get a new job should they lose the one they have. In short, they must be trained not only to be employable but also *re*employable.

These needs highlight both strengths and weaknesses in the German and American systems that together provide an opportunity for a bilateral initiative on learning and competitiveness—a fifth step toward building new economic ties. Such an initiative can build new coalitions across the Atlantic. It can strengthen the bilateral relationship at the same time it advances our economic and educational goals.

The key is to focus on the non-college bound. The U.S. educational system is geared to preparing young people for college. But 79 percent of all Americans never get an undergraduate degreee. The skills of the non-college bound—the vast majority of the American workforce—are an essential foundation for national competitiveness. But the United States does not even have a system of post-secondary skill training that helps them make the transition from classroom to workplace. That translates into lost productivity and wasted human potential.

The German "dual" training system, on the other hand, where vocational or practical and academic training is combined, is widely regarded as one of the keys to German economic prowess. The dual system is an integral part of the German social market economy that has delivered high wages and high productivity. It has helped maintain German competitiveness despite some of the highest production costs in the world.

About 70 percent of students completing school—at various levels —go into training in the dual system, which covers a wide range of industrial and service professions. No particular degree or certificate is required to enter the dual system, and training lasts between two and three and a half years. The "dual" aspect is the combination of workplace or on the job training with classroom vocational education. Typically, one or two days a week is spent in the classroom, where 60 percent of the instruction is vocationally oriented and 40 percent is general education. The government pays for the classroom costs and provides other subsidies. Local chambers of commerce accredit instructors and organize the standardized exams that trainees have to pass to qualify for certification.

The joint government-industry program trains 65 percent of the country's work force. The system works well for workers who are less academically oriented and who are eager to enter the workforce at an early age. Youth unemployment is kept low. By contrast, only 3 percent of American men and 1 percent of women are in an apprentice program by age 25.

The dual system is costly: businesses pump 2 percent of their payroll into training—a total of about DM 50 billion a year. It is also tightly regulated. But government largely confines itself to giving legal force to training programs negotiated between employers and unions industry by industry.

Although a company must be certified to provide dual training, virtually all eligible firms in Germany participate. In part this is because of the access to trained workers the system provides (some 41 percent of apprentices stay on with their training company) but also because it provides a cheap labor source. Average apprentice wages are around DM 750 month, less than $500.

The German training system is part of an overall education and social system which is very different from that in the United States. There is far more stratification in the German school system.

The dual training system excels at developing skilled industrial labor that employers find valuable. It is an important mechanism easing the transition from school to work. But it is less well-suited to creating a path to management positions. Moreover, in open, dynamic economies increasingly characterized by significant job turnover, individuals who are the product of a system that emphasizes a specific set of work skills could find it harder to get reemployed than individuals who have more general skills or have been trained to be flexible and adaptable to changing competitive conditions.

But even here there may be something to learn. Under the German system, unemployment benefits and what Americans call welfare are a last resort. Counseling, training and retraining, active job placement, incentives to employers for the maintenance and creation of jobs, and wage subsidies and payments to employers to keep people they would otherwise lay off—all these measures are used before welfare and unemployment provisions are invoked.

In Germany competing businesses join hands to train workers to top standards, rather than the narrow needs of individual companies,

THE AREA OF LEARNING AND COMPETITIVENESS OFFERS RICH OPPORTUNITIES FOR COLLABORATION BETWEEN AMERICAN STATES AND GERMAN *LÄNDER*.

without any guarantee that the worker they train will in fact join their company. This could be difficult for American business to accept. In Germany 50 percent of apprentices who start with one company end up with another, and 50 percent end up in a different field.

Thus there are reasons why it would be both difficult and probably undesirable to graft the German system onto American education. Simply transplanting the German approach could give Americans a system that costs more and performs less well. Moreover, national or even state systems of school-to-work transition are unlikely to address more fundamental problems such as functional illiteracy, lack of rudimentary mathematical skills or the pervasive influence of drugs and violence in America's schools.

But clearly there are elements that could be adapted profitably to American conditions. The challenge is to discover how to take the best of the German system and combine it with the best of the American system.

The weaknesses of the German system also demonstrate that the issue of learning and competitiveness is not just one-way. There is a growing recognition in Germany that the dual system needs to be streamlined, the quality of training must be improved, rigidities have to be cleared away. New forms of work organization developed by Germany's major competitors question how well Germany's entrenched hierarchies of skill can adapt to the rigors of global competition, which require supple structures and fluid relationships. There is an urgent need to promote female participation and deal with questions of diversity in the workplace.

Many of Germany's deficiencies are America's strengths. The average American will change jobs seven times in his or her lifetime. The United States has a far more fluid, mobile labor market than does Germany. This sets the stage for a two-way exchange in a way that would not have been likely only a few years ago.

Moreover, key actors now appear willing to consider a more concerted bilateral initiative. More German companies in the United States favor such programs. In the late 1970s the German company Stihl implemented an intensive four-year apprentice program at its Virginia subsidiary that has helped the company triple worker productivity. Such German companies as Siemens America, BMW and Philip Holtzman are already exploring or have implemented apprentice training programs in the U.S. Others could well be persuaded to participate in pilot programs to improve their own worker productivity and their ties to the communities in which they have invested.

The German government has also focused on the possibilities of a bilateral initiative on training. The federal Economics Ministry is already considering a program to sponsor experts' exchanges and coordinate an approach to the German private sector. In the German private sector a bilateral initiative could include the German Association of Chambers of Commerce (DIHT), which maintains trade offices in the U.S. and which could provide possible financial support. More intensive relations between German and American trade and business associations could be an important benefit.

Perhaps most important, the Clinton Administration is earmarking $1 billion over three years through the School to Work Opportunities Act to help create school-to-work transition programs. In its fiscal year 1994 budget, the administration asked for $270 million to initiate a national system for school-to-work transition. The money is only a fraction of the funds already available through the Labor Department for transition programs and worker training. In August 1993 the administration submitted a more comprehensive legislative proposal that would provide grants for states to establish school-to-work systems and additional help for states and localities that already have such programs.

Because the Clinton Administration has devolved responsibility for policy initiatives to the states, this is a rich area of opportunity for federal-state cooperation and state-to-state relations between German and American states. Ten states are already trying school-to-work transition programs modeled in part on German and Danish experiences. Rather than being neutral observers, national governments can be active facilitators of a mutual exchange of experience. The German Länder could be brought into this exchange. U.S. private sector participation could include the U.S. Chamber of Commerce, trade associations, the AFL-CIO and education associations or junior college associations. The Congressional Study Group on Germany could also provide sponsorship for a program of information exchanges. A new initiative should also build on the extensive experience that has already been accumulated. Non-governmental organizations such as the German Marshall Fund and the Carl Duisberg Society have long been active in the field.

Money Matters

Closer coordination of monetary policies is the sixth essential element of a new transatlantic bargain. Improving the compatibility of monetary and fiscal policies among the members of the G-7 is more necessary than ever before. Stable economic growth in the Triad requires smoother movement of exchange rates between the dollar, *Deutsche Mark* and yen. This in turn depends on the nature of European monetary integration. The United States must position itself to influence that process so that it strengthens rather than weakens G-7 coordination.

Such a proposal stands in stark contrast to fashionable arguments of the moment. Gloaters argue that closer European monetary union is a pipe dream; gloomers argue that U.S. influence is minimal. Both are wrong. The combination of recession, high German interest rates and successive currency upheavals may have damaged the Maastricht timetable of achieving monetary union by 1999, but Europeans understand that a zone of monetary stability is indispensable to their prosperity. Despite the fact that the Exchange Rate Mechanism now permits wider bands of fluctuation between member currencies, national monetary authorities have avoided competitive currency devaluations and most have chosen to remain within the old, tighter bands in relation to the *Deutsche Mark*. Even if one accepts the view that monetary union will never come about, new consultative mechanisms could at a minimum improve coordination both among the major monetary powers and between fiscal and monetary policies in leading economies such as Germany and the United States.

The creation of a European Central Bank at the heart of a single European economic and monetary union carries fundamental implications for the United States. As the EU develops a single currency— and continues to make changes toward that eventual goal—the role of the dollar in global markets could change dramatically. The European Currency Unit could challenge the place of the dollar as the world's leading currency. The terms of the U.S. government's debt financing would be further constrained. Monetary union would block

FAILURE TO AGREE ON APPROPRIATE PRIORITIES OF FISCAL AND MONETARY POLICY COULD BECOME ONE OF THE MOST CONTENTIOUS ASPECTS OF THE RELATIONSHIP.

Washington's ability to use rapid changes in the value of the dollar to pressure European governments to boost domestic demand.

Moreover, an inward-looking European Union may favor internal exchange rate stabilization over G-7 cooperation. If the European Bank adopts German monetary principles—the sine qua non of German willingness to give up the *Deutsche Mark*—European monetary union will, on the whole, exert a deflationary influence on the global economy.

Washington has been curiously passive. When the Europeans make moves toward an independent military force, U.S. officials swarm all over the idea. When the Europeans make moves toward an independent monetary force, U.S. officials yawn. But the nature of European monetary integration is already having tangible effects on U.S. economic welfare. When the *Bundesbank* raised German interest rates in the wake of unification, they radiated through Europe's rigid exchange rate mechanism. This caused interest rates to rise across the continent. Europe's subsequent slowdown dragged down U.S. economic prospects. This could be only a taste of things to come.

The transition to monetary union will be an important formative experience for monetary officials in Europe who will later be in charge of common policies. It is important to engage them now. Major questions remain open. For instance, how flexible is the European Union likely to be on questions of exchange rate stabilization? Will it be inclined to invoke capital controls? Will the key decisionmaking body be the Committee of Central Bank Governors or the European Monetary Institute? What is the relationship of either to the Council of Ministers?

Europeans themselves have not resolved these crucial issues. This provides an opportunity for the United States to reinvigorate G-7 fiscal and monetary coordination while the European monetary scene remains fluid, molding it as much as possible as it firms so that it does not harden into something to our disliking. If European monetary authorities come to believe G-7 coordination can be effective, monetary union could enhance multilateral cooperation. If, however, the G-7 parties continue to deflect responsibility for macroeconomic policy adjustments onto one another, European monetary authorities will be more likely to take a dim, narrow view of international coopera-

WHEN THE EUROPEANS MAKE MOVES TOWARD AN INDEPENDENT MILITARY FORCE, U.S. OFFICIALS SWARM ALL OVER THE IDEA. WHEN THE EUROPEANS MAKE MOVES TOWARD AN INDEPENDENT MONETARY FORCE, U.S. OFFICIALS YAWN.

tion. Monetary union could mar prospects for broader coordination and damage important U.S. domestic economic priorities.

Two proposals might help. One is substantive, the other procedural. First, it may be profitable to seek a G-7 agreement to work together to limit excessive exchange rate fluctuations, without impinging on central bank independence, by setting up broad target zones within which major currencies could fluctuate. Central banks jealous of their autonomy might resist such a proposal. But interdependence has rendered full monetary autonomy an illusion. The independence that is lost through exchange rate stabilization could mean authority regained, since it could enhance the ability of central banks to base monetary policies on a widely agreed upon and predictable set of parameters and margins of fluctuation. This is essentially the model offered by the European monetary system: Governments decide the parities and margins of fluctuation, and the central banks work within them. Even the fiercely independent *Bundesbank* agreed to this because it had an opt-out proviso in case of extreme disruption. Such a proviso could be incorporated into the new G-7 framework.

Such a step would be quite demanding and is certainly no panacea. The tremendous speculative waves that mark the new global economy render the traditional buffering role of central banks vastly more difficult. Moreover, successful macroeconomic policy coordination is unlikely to result simply from better coordination of exchange rates; underlying macroeconomic forces play a much more important role. But an initiative on exchange rates could be of modest value in moderating currency swings.

Second, central bank sensitivities could be further assuaged, and coordination between fiscal and monetary policies enhanced both within nations and between them by including finance and central bank officials at the working "deputies" level during the preparatory work leading to G-7 sessions.

Germany's position could be decisive. Until a European central monetary authority is set up, European monetary policy will be set by the *Bundesbank*. It is likely to lean toward a cautious policy during most of the decade because it will want to leave a legacy of monetary stability to its successor. It is in U.S. interests to see that it leaves another legacy: that of intense and profitable G-7 coordination.

A New Vision

The initiatives that are proposed here—flexible "dialogue mechanisms" between senior working level U.S. and EU authorities; microeconomic compacts; cooperation on learning and competitiveness; closer monetary coordination; "sensitive sector" working groups that consider the transatlantic consequences of EU enlargement; and consultative mechanisms between NAFTA, the EEA and APEC—can set the stage for a more ambitious vision: the creation, sometime in the next century, of a single transatlantic market. A single transatlantic market incorporating members of the North American Free Trade Area and the European Economic Area would be a fulcrum of global economic growth. It would provide rich opportunities for enhanced trade, investment and jobs. Its dispute-dampening mechanisms would ensure that economic and monetary tensions did not undercut the transatlantic strategic relationship. It would create a broader base for an American role in Europe that would be both profitable and sustainable.

Such a goal is ambitious; it may never be achieved. Even its pursuit, however, could have salutary effects for transatlantic security and economic welfare. There is no need to have an answer to this question now in order to get started on manageable pieces of the policy. The journey can be as important as the destination. Simply adopting the objective itself would strengthen U.S. market-opening goals. Such goals could be pursued in graduated ways that would not be excessively disruptive. They would spur deeper U.S.-EU negotiations and mechanisms on more ambitious objectives over a protracted period of time. Concerted efforts would be required to keep the economic peace in ways that strengthened multilateral arrangements. The point is that the vision need not be limited by current understandings of political feasibility. As the new transatlantic regime is strengthened, as existing barriers fall and momentum builds, the boundaries of what seems feasible are likely to expand. We should pursue practical steps, but toward visionary objectives. The point is to enunciate the goal and get the process started. Germany and the United States can show the way.

Beyond Bonn

A Strategic Environmental Initiative

During the forty years the industrialized world was preoccupied with the Cold War, the human species caused more change to the planet than it had in the previous ten thousand years. It took thousands of generations for the earth's population to reach 2 billion; it will take one lifetime for it to go from 2 to 6 billion. Revolutions in science and technology have brought untold benefits to billions of people. But population growth, economic progress and technological advance have combined to produce faster, more extensive and more unpredictable global change than any the planet has experienced since the arrival of humankind.

In the post-Wall world global menaces to European and American ways of life loom large. Yet these threats are not unleashed by governments, but by forces of nature, masses of humanity, unsustainable growth—by the billions of individual decisions that people make every day. So leadership must begin with understanding.

Rapid population growth, stratospheric ozone depletion, tropical deforestation, greenhouse warming, regional water pollution and acid rain share certain characteristics. They pose potentially serious dangers to human health and national wealth. They are ignorant of political and ideological borders. They question traditional notions of security. And as we have seen with the new world's other security and economic challenges, they will either be dealt with collectively or they will not be dealt with at all.

There are opportunities. Environmental imperatives are pushing the world into a new economic era. Environmental efficiency is fast becoming a key element of global competitiveness. A $200 billion global environmental technology industry has emerged that is likely to triple over the course of the decade.[2] Technologies, concepts and ways of doing business that make products and production processes more environmentally efficient are likely to form the industrial infrastructure of the twenty-first century.

This means shifting economic activity away from technologies that control and clean up pollution after the fact to green technologies that prevent pollution from occurring in the first place. Investments in such new technologies improve environmental quality while improving competitiveness. The gains in efficiency provide a long-term competitive advantage even in products and processes not normally connected to the environment. As a result, the environmental market, once limited largely to add-on pollution control devices, is expanding steadily to encompass most products and processes.

A German-American Strategic Partnership

For decades the United States and Germany applied their best strategic thinking to issues of deterrence and containment. There is a clear need today to apply that sort of thinking to the strategic challenges posed by humankind's relations with the environment.

Germany and the United States are uniquely suited to be engines of multilateral change. Even though they are both major polluters— the U.S. produces more waste and Germany exports more waste than any other nation—they are also important environmental leaders and innovators. Both have developed leading-edge technologies to deal with environmental degradation and adopted stiff regulations to limit environmental damage arising from their economic activities. Both stand as global leaders in education, science and technological prowess. An intense transatlantic exchange on ecological sciences and environmental practices occurs between non-governmental organizations in both countries. Research on climate and energy conservation by American scientists has probably influenced the climate policy and energy policy debate in Europe more than in the United States itself. The German *Bundestag*'s Enquete Commission investigation of dangers to the earth's atmosphere fueled environmental

Chart 7

**World Market
for Environmental
Technology**

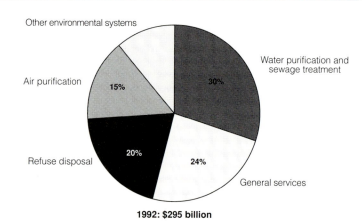

Other environmental systems

Water purification and
sewage treatment

Air purification

15%

30%

Refuse disposal

20%

24%

General services

1992: $295 billion

Source: Commerzbank; U.S. Department of Commerce

and scientific debate in the United States. Public opinion in both countries gives priority to the environment.

Germany has taken a variety of environmental initiatives at the national, regional and global level. German leadership was essential to multilateral agreement to reduce sulphur dioxide and nitrogen emissions. Germany has already reduced drastically its consumption of chlorofluorocarbons (CFCs) and by the end of 1994 is likely to be the first industrialized country to have banned use of CFCs completely. It has been driving the international community toward binding commitments to reduce CO_2 emissions and has already begun to do so at home. It has spurred a variety of regional and global agreements on hazardous wastes. Germany's environmental expenditure as a percentage of GDP and its share of public R&D monies devoted to environmental purposes are among the highest in the Organization for Economic Cooperation and Development (OECD). Germany's approach is crucial within the European Union. It pushed its European partners to adopt the Montreal Protocol and to adopt catalyst-based emission standards for motor vehicles. Chancellor Kohl pushed successfully to put the environment on the permanent agenda of the G-7.

Moreover, Germany has been able to *decouple* economic growth from the flow of several major pollutants—a necessary and important step towards sustainable economic growth. West Germany's GDP rose by 23 percent during the 1980s while its SO_2 emissions fell by 71 percent and particulate emissions dropped 35 percent. German firms are world leaders with exports of DM 35 billion and a 21 percent

Chart 8

Environmental Industry in Selected Countries, 1990

	Production (Billion US$)	Export Share (%)[a]	Employment (x 1000)
western Germany	27.0	40.0	320
United States	80.0	10.0	800
Japan	30.0	6.0	200
France	12.0	14.0	90
United Kingdom	9.0	17.0	75

[a]Percentage of production exported
Source: OECD

share of global exports of environmental technology. Germany's "eco-industry" has generated 320,000 jobs. Economic efficiencies aimed at cleaning up the environment are expected to become the basis of German economic competitiveness over the next century. Germany shows that cleaning up industry is not an impediment to commerce but a stimulant. Rigorous environmental requirements have yielded a wide range of technological advances, many of which are now exported to other nations.

For decades the U.S. set the pace in establishing institutions and regulations to halt and reverse damage to the environment. The U.S. approach to environmental protection, which included such innovations as environmental impact assessment, originally was the model for many nations. In the 1980s other nations took the lead in several key areas such as climate change and policy planning. But the United States continues to innovate. Unnoticed by most, it has developed important new instruments for reducing toxic emissions, including the Toxic Release Inventory and a related program of voluntary reductions. 45,000–60,000 mostly small- to medium-sized companies are active in the U.S. environmental industry. U.S. companies have captured 16 percent of the global export market for environmental technology.

A German-American strategic initiative to mobilize scientific and managerial talent to confront the strategic challenge of the environment would provide the high-level political support in the European Union needed to mobilize collective action. Moreover, there is a new need to cooperate. On a variety of issues ranging from toxics and standards to the relationship between trade and the environment, America's string of bilateral relations with individual EU members no longer suffices and the OECD is too diffuse. The environment is becoming a shared area of competence between EU member nations and the European Commission in Brussels. The U.S.-EU dialogue will set the global environmental agenda—either by driving it forward or by holding it back.

Political momentum is lacking. A German-American spark could jumpstart the transatlantic debate. It could fulfill other U.S. goals toward Germany as well, such as creating new coalitions, encouraging Germany to consider its broader global responsibilities and ensuring that the European Union look outward.

Close German-American collaboration was decisive in the international effort to ban CFCs—an example of how the bilateral motor can drive multilateral action. A German-American environmental partnership could lend political momentum in two important areas.

A High Level Environmental Working Group

The best first step would be to push for a high-profile U.S.-EU working group to examine policy areas where concerted transatlantic action is needed most urgently: climate policy, protecting forests and biodiversity, restructuring development cooperation and recommending changes in the U.N. system and in the multilateral banking system. The group would work with national foreign aid agencies to make sustainable development one of the key objectives of European and American foreign aid. It would recommend new policies and procedures to bring environmental concerns into the mainstream of the U.S.-EU dialogue. It would come up with ways to drive forward the agenda of the U.N. Commission on Sustainable Development. As Europe's central environmental player, Germany will be essential to launch this group.

A U.S.-EU exchange is as necessary for those who are seeking a more resolute approach to environmental protection as for those who worry about its costs, trade effects, scientific justification or economic impact. Both the United States and the EU have an interest in pooling resources, exchanging information and promoting scientific consen-

Chart 9		Kilotons	Kilograms per capita
Export of Hazardous Wastes, 1990	Germany (western)	522.1	8.26
	Canada	137.8	5.18
	United States	118.4	0.47
	Italy	20.0	0.35
	France	10.5	0.19
	United Kingdom	0.5	0.01
	Japan	0.0	0.00

Source: OECD

ECONOMIC GROWTH IS ESSENTIAL, BUT IT IS THE *KIND* OF GROWTH, NOT THE SHEER *AMOUNT*, THAT IS CRITICAL— THE QUALITY, NOT ONLY THE QUANTITY.

sus in this area. Given limited resources and competition for government funds, neither side of the Atlantic has an interest in duplicating the other's efforts. Better use could be made of non-governmental organizations, research institutions and market-based approaches on both sides of the Atlantic.

Sorting Out the Right Answers

The most significant new age hurdles, however, are in areas where the challenge is not to generate sufficient political will to implement widely agreed upon goals, but to sort through issues where the right answers are not yet clear. This is a second area where the German-American engine might accelerate thinking. There are at least four such topics: the practical workaday implications of adopting a policy of sustainable development; tangled tradeoffs between environment and trade; managing environmental problems caused by chemicals; and the implications for policy posed by scientific uncertainty in the face of potentially irreversible change. A final area where bilateral cooperation might prove mutually beneficial is precompetitive research into the commercialization of environmental technology.

Unlocking the Secret of Sustainable Development

We have a chance of moving beyond the rather sterile debate between the "limits to growth—no growth" school and the "growth at all costs" school by examining seriously the concept of sustainable development. It rests on what should be a fairly uncontroversial principle in the eyes of either school: The most efficient form of economic activity uses the fewest resources to achieve its purpose. In this regard there are two big opportunities and two big challenges.

Our first opportunity is to accept the notion that economic growth is essential, but that it is the *kind* of growth, not the sheer *amount*, that is critical—the quality, not only the quantity. Sound environmental management must be a component of economic growth, not an afterthought. Although there are difficult short-term tradeoffs, it is now widely recognized that long-term environmental and economic health are more often mutually dependent than conflicting. Without economic growth nations are less likely to conserve natural resources that may have global benefits. Growth enables countries to reorder costs and priorities so that environmental considerations can be integrated into economic decisionmaking. Our first challenge is to translate this approach into useful ways of doing business.

The second challenge is the concept's ideological baggage. All too quickly "sustainable development" is viewed almost exclusively as a North-South issue. In essential ways, of course, this is true. Even if all the industrialized countries of the world halve their emissions of SO_2 within the next seven years and only two countries—India and China—continue to develop their coal-burning programs, global SO_2 emissions are likely to double. But clean growth is not simply a North-South issue. It is a crucial issue within the North. Unless there is sustainable growth in the North, and some rudimentary agreement among the major economies about how this may be achieved, there is little prospect of sustainable development in the South.

Our second opportunity, then, is to launch a concerted effort with-

Chart 10

Selected Environmental Data[a]: Air

	Germany	western Germany	eastern Germany	USA	Japan	OECD[d]
Emissions of sulphur oxides (kg/cap.)	71.7	14.9	292.9	84.3	6.9	49.4
" (kg/1000 US$ GDP)[b]	..	1.0	..	4.7	0.6	3.5
Emissions of nitrogen oxides (kg/cap.)	40.7	41.2	38.7	78.3	9.7	44.7
" (kg/1000 US$ GDP)[b]	..	2.7	..	4.3	0.8	3.1
Emissions of carbon dioxide (t./cap.)[c]	13.1	11.3	20.1	20.0	8.6	12.0
" (t./1000 US$ GDP)[b]	..	0.74	..	1.10	0.58	0.84

.. = Not available.
[a] Data refer to 1990 or the latest available year. Data are provisional.
[b] GDP at 1985 prices and PPPs
[c] CO_2 from energy use only; international marine bunkers included.
[d] Includes western Germany only.
Source: OECD

UNDER CURRENT METHODS
OF CALCULATING GNP A
COUNTRY'S ECONOMIC
"GROWTH" RECEIVES
A DOUBLE BOOST FROM
PRODUCTION OF TOXIC
PRODUCTS AND FROM THEIR
SUBSEQUENT COSTLY
CLEANUP.

in the North to unlock some practical, policy-relevant aspects of sustainable development.

For economic growth to be sustainable, prices must be made to reflect the costs of environmental as well as other resources. Open, competitive markets are the most effective way of meeting human needs. But at present market prices frequently do not adequately integrate environmental costs into economic decisions—by either business or government. We should now begin to consider these costs as integral, rather than external, to the way we conduct our business.

The shifts required in business practices, government policies, and consumer attitudes to reflect a new understanding of "full-cost pricing" pose a major challenge within and between countries. Such an approach, even if it produces a net social gain, will provoke stiff opposition because it will alter the mixture of economic winners and losers. The core issue is to identify policies that can ease the transition to more sustainable business practices and thus to more sustainable economies. This is an area where domestic and foreign policies intersect, where current practices are outmoded, and where no nation has a monopoly on wisdom.

A few examples indicate where changes could be sought. Reforming aggregate measures of economic performance in national accounts such as GNP would be useful. Under current methods of calculating GNP a country's economic "growth" receives a double boost from production of toxic products and from their subsequent costly cleanup. The more that countries such as Indonesia and Malaysia destroy their tropical forests, the more "growth" they register in the GNP. At the individual business level, the technique of present value discounting intrinsically underestimates future harm while predisposing managers toward investment decisions that maximize short-run profits. Better use could also be made of economic incentives such as tradeable permits and pollution charges to encourage least-cost solutions that use rather than abuse the market.

Efforts at reform are fraught with difficulty. There are limits to efforts to "price the earth." One cannot price the protection of a whale or determine what the world is willing to pay for a slightly used stratospheric ozone layer. But simply that environmental costs are so hard to estimate is no argument for abandoning the effort. First, setting a rough value may be a better basis for policy than none at all—only by groping for values for environmental resources can governments and businesses think sensibly about costs and benefits. Second, such efforts can discourage perverse economic signals that encourage passing on costs rather than carrying them. Third, the business and financial communities have already moved beyond the inconclusive scholarly debate. Environmental concerns have become a strategic part of business and investment decisions. Upstream solutions that anticipate and design out potential environmental problems are catching on more quickly in major chemical companies than in federal regulatory agencies.

There is much ferment at many levels in the clean production and materials area for both environmental and economic reasons. Putting these interests together is what sustainable development is all about. German-American networks of environmental, business, academic and governmental leaders could play an important role. The newly formed German American Academic Council could be a useful catalyst by promoting collaborative research schemes that create lasting interdisciplinary networks in this area.

The Environment and Trade

This issue is of particular relevance to transatlantic relations not just because of weighty trade ties and the burgeoning global environ-

Chart 11

Selected Environmental Data[a]: Waste Generated

	Germany	western Germany	eastern Germany	USA	Japan	OECD[d]
Industrial waste (kg/1000 US$ GDP)[b]	..	70	..	184	189	122
Municipal waste (kg/cap.)	352	335	418	803	406	509
Nuclear waste (t./Mtoe of TPES)[c]	..	1.8	..	1.2	1.6	1.9

.. = Not available.
[a] Data refer to 1990 or the latest available year. Data are provisional.
[b] GDP at 1985 prices and PPPs
[c] Waste from spent fuel in nuclear power plants, in tons of heavy metal per million tons of oil equivalent (total primary energy supply)
[d] Includes western Germany only.
Source: OECD

THE ENVIRONMENT IS NOT SIMPLY ANOTHER TRADE BARRIER. IT IS OF A FUNDAMENTALLY DIFFERENT QUALITY. CONNECTIONS WITH TRADE CUT IN DIFFERENT WAYS.

mental market, but because the European Union has increasing competence over the environment, and this is likely to be the most urgent issue on the post–Uruguay Round trade agenda.

There is much talk of a new "Green Round" for the GATT that deals with the relationship between environment and trade. But it is unclear when and if a "Green Round" would actually be launched and what its mandate would be. It assumes that the GATT will continue to operate as before—an unlikely proposition after the exhausting and aggravating Uruguay Round. It also assumes that environmental issues are amenable to the kind of negotiation the trade rounds represent—another questionable notion.

A "Green Round" requires significant intellectual groundwork if it is ever to be launched. The environment is not simply another trade barrier. It is of a fundamentally different quality. Connections with trade cut in different ways. High environmental standards can expand exports by stimulating innovation or can curb them by imposing higher costs or by being used as a pretext for protectionism. Freer trade could improve environmental management or encourage short-sighted plunder of natural resources. The current situation is not acceptable, but the right answers are in short supply. In what circumstances is it legitimate to use trade measures to protect the environment outside national jurisdiction? Which should take precedence—an international environment agreement or the GATT?

There is little time to waste. History shows that after every multilateral trade round in the past individual governments have relapsed into protectionism. The bicycle of liberalization and groundrules for trade must continue to move forward. In this context a German-American initiative on trade and the environment would be useful. Again the two countries are pivotal as the two top trading nations in the world and the major environmental players. Perhaps GATT members could agree broadly on the importance of the question and begin talks as soon as possible, drafting principles to govern the relationship between environment and trade. It is not possible to get all the details right today, but a broad conceptual initiative would be useful.

Cleaner Chemicals

German and American chemical companies are the global leaders in their industry. If there is to be a move to more cost-effective manage-

GERMAN AND AMERICAN CHEMICAL COMPANIES ARE THE GLOBAL LEADERS IN THEIR INDUSTRY. IF THERE IS TO BE A MOVE TO MORE COST-EFFECTIVE MANAGEMENT OF ENVIRONMENTAL PROBLEMS CAUSED BY CHEMICALS, IT WILL HAVE TO BEGIN WITH GERMANY AND THE UNITED STATES.

ment of environmental problems caused by chemicals, it will have to begin with Germany and the United States.

The chemical industry has taken a leading role in German industry's overall contribution to improving the environment. Very large investments have been made and pollutants have been reduced quickly. The principle of preventive action has been implemented through various notification and assessment programs. Greater use of risk analysis and of the life-cycle concept in the chemical sector should also make a contribution. Issues remain, however, that could be tackled through German-American collaboration:

- *Environmental performance reporting.* At the moment, the United States requires companies to report to the public the release and transfers to waste management facilities of about 320 chemicals. The European Union is developing a new environmental reporting system. While the system is voluntary, German companies will be required by insurance companies to participate. A German-American project on environmental reporting, perhaps sponsored by the German-American Academic Council, could spark the broader international standard-setting process while driving improvements in both economic efficiency and environmental protection. It might encourage more transparency in German decisionmaking and give Americans an opportunity to learn from German progress in environmental accounting.

- *Policies for spurring green products.* A project could focus directly on policies to encourage green products. The Germans have a real lead in areas such as take-back requirements, research, labeling, and ecobalances. An ambitious Enquete Commission on sustainable development in chemical substances, raw materials and emissions to the environment has been established. A partner commission in the United States could facilitate such efforts with benefits for both countries.

- *Steps toward an international chemicals convention.* It is in the interests of the U.S. and Germany as major producers to have international standards on chemicals. In recent years chemical companies in OECD countries have been very concerned with Korea's approach to screening new chemicals, which they view as a trade barrier and fear could be adopted by other countries. Moreover, both countries are beginning to be pressured from inside as well as outside by newer interests: businesses and consumers who primarily use rather than manufacture chemicals and by environmental interests whether in government, business or non-governmental organizations. A new Intergovernmental Forum on Chemicals is likely to meet for the first time in Stockholm in April 1994 to prepare the June 1994 meeting of the Commission on Sustainable Development on toxics issues. A German-American initiative that would convert and extend current OECD guidelines on chemicals testing into an international chemicals convention could show the way.

Investigating the Precautionary Principle

What should the United States and the international community do when faced with scientific uncertainty regarding environmental phenomena and the knowledge that if we wait until we have certainty it could be too late to reverse change? The possibility of irreversible change on a global scale is the distinguishing characteristic of the most pressing of these phenomena. Nature does not send conve-

Chart 12

Energy Supply[a]

	Germany	western Germany	eastern Germany	USA	Japan	OECD[b]
Total supply (Mtoe)	367	278	89	1906	428	3985
% change (1980–1990)	1.2	1.9	-1.2	5.8	23.9	10.0
Energy intensity (Toe/1000 US$)	..	0.3	..	0.4	0.2	0.3
% change (1980–1990)	..	-17.4	..	-17.2	-17.5	-15.7
Structure of energy supply (%)						
Solid fuels	38.8	27.5	74.3	27.4	17.3	24.2
Oil	34.9	40.9	16.2	39.7	58.2	42.9
Gas	15.0	17.3	7.6	22.9	10.1	20.6
Nuclear	10.8	13.8	1.6	9.0	8.4	10.6
Hydro, etc.	0.4	0.5	0.1	1.7	2.1	2.9

.. = Not available.
[a] Data refer to 1990 and to the period 1980-1990. Data are provisional.
[b] Includes western Germany only.
Source: OECD

WHAT SHOULD THE UNITED STATES AND THE INTERNATIONAL COMMUNITY DO WHEN FACED WITH SCIENTIFIC UNCERTAINTY REGARDING ENVIRONMENTAL PHENOMENA *AND* THE KNOWLEDGE THAT IF WE WAIT UNTIL WE HAVE CERTAINTY IT COULD BE TOO LATE TO REVERSE CHANGE?

nient early warning signals. It may not be possible to know when environmental breakdown can no longer be repaired. There may be a need to take action before the scientific evidence is conclusive.

Examples abound. When the Montreal protocol was negotiated, the evidence on CFCs was as uncertain as today's evidence on global warming. But countries still agreed to set the goals. Even so, it will take a century to reverse the current damage to the ozone.

The same processes and dangers apply to CO_2 emissions. Mainstream scientific consensus tells us that CO_2 emissions are a dangerous problem. The real question is when to act. If we wait too long, the costs could be enormous and the damage perhaps irreversible.

The notion that there may be a need to take precautionary action before there is scientific certainty is widely viewed as a "loose cannon," a policy principle that opens the door to arbitrary decisions. A German-American initiative to make more policy-relevant use of the precautionary principle could prove useful.

• • •

These are only a few suggestions where concerted German-American action could make a contribution. Public and private organizations could be tapped to work more effectively together in these areas. Whether Germany and the United States decide to join forces to mobilize broad new coalitions on environmental issues is primarily a matter of political priority.

The United States and the Berlin Republic

Defining conditions of the Cold War partnership have either disappeared or changed fundamentally. Germans and Americans are less tightly bound by a unifying security threat. This may make joint action harder, but it does not make it less necessary.

Failure to align U.S. and German policies does not preclude success for American objectives in Europe and globally, but it will make those goals far more difficult to achieve. If Germany and the United States, together with their partners, are to drive the democracies forward, the character of the relationship must change to reflect new realities. Whether Americans have the patience to assemble the type of coalitions recommended here and whether Germans will develop the broader understanding of their responsibilities that must underpin such coalitions are open questions that will test leadership in both countries.

The United States is unlikely to change its ways unless the European Union does so as well. The danger is that each side points to the other to justify why it is not they but others who have to change. As so often in the past, the nature of the German-American partnership could prove decisive.

•   •   •

ENDNOTES

1. Statistical information presented in this chapter is drawn from the European-American Chamber of Commerce in Washington, D.C., Inc., *The United States and Europe: Jobs, Trade and Investment* (Washington, D.C., July 1993); *Europe*, September and October 1993; and Deutsche Bank AG. Investment figures are from the Bureau of Economic Analysis, U.S. Department of Commerce; export-related job figures are the author's own calculations based on the above sources and the Massachusetts Institute for Social and Economic Research (MISER) at the University of Massachusetts. Other sources include 1991 and 1993 World Population Data Sheet, published by the Population Reference Bureau; State of Baden-Württemberg; *Arbeitskreis deutsche Länder*; William Lewis, "The Secret to Competitiveness," *The Wall Street Journal*, October 22, 1993; *Business Week*, July 19, l993; *Financial Times*, October 11, 1993; and Dan Price, "Pitfalls of Prioritizing Recipients of U.S. Government Support," unpublished draft discussion paper, July 21, 1993.

2. Environmental statistics used in this chapter are drawn from Organization for Economic Cooperation and Development, *OECD Environmental Performance Reviews: Germany* (Paris: OECD, 1993); U.S. Government Interagency Environmental Technologies Exports Working Group, *Environmental Technologies Exports: Strategic Framework for U.S. Leadership* (Washington, D.C., November 1993); and Commerzbank.

Participants in the Study Group

Chairman
Steven Muller
Co-Chairman, American Institute for Contemporary German Studies. President Emeritus, the Johns Hopkins University, and Distinguished Professorial Lecturer, Paul H. Nitze School of Advanced International Studies, Johns Hopkins University.

Director
Daniel Hamilton
Senior Associate, Carnegie Endowment for International Peace. Coordinator, Carnegie Endowment National Commission on America and the New World; Coordinator, Commission on Government Renewal; Former Deputy Director, Aspen Institute Berlin.

Peter F. Allgeier
Assistant U.S. Trade Representative for Europe and the Mediterranean. Former Assistant U.S. Trade Representative for Asia and the Pacific.

Michael A. Almond
Partner and Chairman of the International Division, Parker, Poe, Adams & Bernstein, Charlotte, North Carolina. Former Visiting Lecturer, University of North Carolina at Chapel Hill School of Law.

Ronald D. Asmus
Senior Political Scientist, International Policy Department, RAND Corporation. Former Senior Research Analyst, Radio Free Europe/Radio Liberty, Inc.

Donald K. Bandler
Senior Foreign Service Officer, U.S. Department of State. Former acting Deputy Chief of Mission, Minister-Counselor for Political and Legal Affairs, U.S. Embassy, Bonn, Germany.

C. Fred Bergsten
Director, Institute for International Economics; Chairman, Competitiveness Policy Council. Former Assistant Secretary of the Treasury for International Affairs.

J. D. Bindenagel
Director, Office of Central European Affairs, U.S. Department of State. Former Deputy Chief of Mission, U.S. Embassy, Berlin, Germany.

Lily Gardner Feldman
Research Director, American Institute for Contemporary German Studies, Johns Hopkins University. Former Associate Professor of Political Science, Tufts University. Author, *The Special Relationship between West Germany and Israel.*

Greg Flynn
Director of Programs, Center for German and European Studies, Georgetown University. Former Senior Associate, Carnegie Endowment for International Peace.

Mark Foulon
Legislative Aide on Foreign Affairs, Office of Senator Bill Bradley. Former Foreign Service Officer and Special Assistant to the Counselor, U.S. Department of State.

Ellen Frost
Counselor to the U.S. Trade Representative, Executive Office of the President. Former Senior Fellow, Institute for International Economics and Washington Representative, United Technologies Corporation.

Jeffrey E. Garten
Under Secretary for International Trade, U.S. Department of Commerce. Former Senior Adviser, The Blackstone Group. Author, *A Cold Peace: America, Japan, Germany and the Struggle for Supremacy.*

Jack Halpern
Louis Block Distinguished Service Professor, University of Chicago; Chairman, German American Academic Council and Vice-President, National Academy of Sciences.

Thomas L. Hughes
President Emeritus, Carnegie Endowment for International Peace. Former Assistant Secretary of State for Intelligence and Research.

Robert M. Kimmitt
Managing Director in investment
banking, Lehman Brothers. Former
U.S. Ambassador to Germany; former
Under Secretary of State for Political
Affairs; former General Counsel, U.S.
Treasury.

Joseph Kruzel
Deputy Assistant Secretary of Defense
for European and NATO Policy.
Former special assistant to the U.S.
Secretary of Defense; former Director,
Program on International Security and
Military Affairs, Ohio State University.

Nelson C. Ledsky
Senior Associate, National Democratic
Institute for International Affairs.
Former U.S. Special Coordinator for
Cyprus; former Chief U.S. Negotiator
for the revision of the NATO Status of
Forces treaty with Germany; former
Special Assistant to the President for
National Security Affairs and Senior
Director for European and Soviet
Affairs.

Kathryn S. Mack
Director, Face-to-Face Program,
Carnegie Endowment for International
Peace. Former Attorney, White &
Case; former Robert Bosch
Foundation Fellow.

Ellen Meade
Economist, Federal Reserve Board.
Author of a variety of articles on U.S.
trade and finance.

John Newhouse
Staff member, *The New Yorker* maga-
zine; Guest Scholar, the Brookings
Institution. Former Assistant Director,
U.S. Arms Control and Disarmament
Agency. Author of books and articles
on European-American relations.

Demetrios G. Papademetriou
Senior Associate and Director,
Immigration Policy Program, Carnegie
Endowment for International Peace;
Chair of the OECD Migration
Committee. Former Director of
Immigration Policy and Research, U.S.
Department of Labor.

Mary Ann Peters
Deputy Assistant Secretary, Bureau of
European and Canadian Affairs, U.S.
Department of State. Former Deputy
Chief of Mission, U.S. Embassy, Sofia,
Bulgaria.

Andrew J. Pierre
Senior Associate, Carnegie
Endowment for International Peace.
Former Director-General, Atlantic
Institute for International Affairs.

Bruce K. Scott
Colonel, U.S. Army; Executive
Assistant to the Vice Chairman, Joint
Chiefs of Staff. Former Commander,
Divisional Engineer Brigade, 1st
Armored Division, Bad Kreuznach,
Germany; former White House Fellow.

James B. Steinberg
Deputy Assistant Secretary for
Regional and Economic Analysis,
Bureau of Intelligence and Research,
U.S. Department of State. Former
Senior Analyst, International Policy
Department, RAND Corporation.

Nancy J. Walker
Foreign Affairs Specialist, Office of
Peacekeeping and Peace
Enforcement Policy, U.S. Department
of Defense. Former German analyst,
Office of Research, U.S. Information
Agency; former Robert Bosch
Foundation Fellow.

Thomas G. Weston
Deputy Assistant Secretary for
European and Canadian Affairs, U.S.
Department of State. Former Deputy
Chief of Mission, U.S. Mission to the
European Communities, Brussels.

Robert B. Zoellick
Executive Vice President and General
Counsel, Fannie Mae. Former
Undersecretary of State for Economic
Affairs; Counselor of the State
Department; Deputy Chief of Staff at
the White House; and Counselor to the
Secretary of the Treasury.

* The opinions expressed in this
essay are those of the author.
The text has been reviewed by
members of the Study Group.
The vast majority agree with the
thrust of the report, but all members do not necessarily endorse
every conclusion, nor does the
report necessarily represent the
views of the organizations with
which the members are affiliated.
During its deliberations, the
Study Group benefited greatly
from the participation of officials
of the U.S. government.
However, their official positions
preclude their identification with
the report.

Appendix: The North Atlantic Treaty

The North Atlantic Treaty

Signed at Washington, D.C. April 4, 1949.
Entered into Force, August 24, 1949.

The Parties to this Treaty reaffirm their faith in the purposes and principles of the Charter of the United Nations and their desire to live in peace with all peoples and all governments.

They are determined to safeguard the freedom, common heritage and civilization of their peoples, founded on the principles of democracy, individual liberty and the rule of law.

They seek to promote stability and well-being in the North Atlantic area.

The are resolved to unite their efforts for collective defense and for the preservation of peace and security.

They therefore agree to this North Atlantic Treaty:

Article 1

The Parties undertake, as set forth in the Charter of the United Nations, to settle any international disputes in which they may be involved by peaceful means in such a manner that international peace and security, and justice, are not endangered, and to refrain in their international relations from the threat or use of force in any manner inconsistent with the purposes of the United Nations.

Article 2

The Parties will contribute toward the further development of peaceful and friendly international relations by strengthening their free institutions, by bringing about a better understanding of the principles upon which these institutions are founded, and by promoting conditions of stability and well-being. They will seek to eliminate conflict in their international economic policies and will encourage economic collaboration between any or all of them.

Article 3

In order more effectively to achieve the objectives of the Treaty, the Parties, separately and jointly, by means of continuous and effective self-help and mutual aid, will maintain and develop their individual and collective capacity to resist armed attack.

Article 4

The Parties will consult together whenever, in the opinion of any of them, the territorial integrity, political independence or security if any of the Parties is threatened.

Article 5

The Parties agree that an armed attack against one or more of them in Europe or North America shall be considered an attack against them all; and consequently they agree that, if such an armed attack occurs, each of them, in exercise of the right of individual or collective self-defense recognized by Article 51 of the Charter of the United Nations, will assist the Party or Parties so attacked by taking forthwith, individually and in concert with the other Parties, such action as it deems necessary, including the use of armed force, to restore and maintain the security of the North Atlantic area.

Any such armed attack and all measures taken as a result thereof shall immediately be reported to the Security Council. Such measures shall be terminated when the Security Council has taken the measures necessary to restore and maintain international peace and security.

Article 6

For the purpose of Article 5 an armed attack on one or more of the Parties is deemed to include an armed attack on the territory of any of the Parties in Europe or North America, on the Algerian departments of France, on the occupation forces of any Party in Europe, on the islands under the jurisdiction of any Party in the North Atlantic area north of the Tropic of Cancer or on the vessels or aircraft in this area of any of the Parties.

Article 7

This Treaty does not affect, and shall not be interpreted as affecting, in any way the rights and obligations under the Charter of the Parties which are members of the United Nations, or the primary responsibility of the Security Council for the maintenance of international peace and security.

Article 8

Each Party declares that none of the international engagements now in force between it and any other of the Parties or any third state is in conflict with the provisions of this Treaty, and undertakes not to enter into any international engagement in conflict with this Treaty.

Article 9

The Parties hereby establish a council, on which each of them shall be represented, to consider matters concerning the implementation of this Treaty. The council shall be so organized as to be able to meet promptly at any time. The council shall set up such subsidiary bodies as may be necessary; in particular it shall establish immediately a defense committee which shall recommend measures for the implementation of Articles 3 and 5.

Article 10

The Parties may, by unanimous agreement, invite any other European state in a position to further the principles of this Treaty and to contribute to the security of the North Atlantic area to accede to this Treaty. Any state so invited may become a party to the Treaty by depositing its instrument of accession with the Government of the United States of America. The Government of the United States of America will inform each of the Parties of the deposit of each such Instrument of accession.

Article 11

This Treaty shall be ratified and its provisions carried out by the Parties in accordance with their respective constitutional processes. The instruments of ratification shall be deposited as soon as possible with the Government of the United States of America, which will notify all the other signatories of each deposit. The Treaty shall enter into force between the states which have ratified it as soon as the ratifications of the majority of the signatories, including the ratifications of Belgium, Canada, France, Luxembourg, the Netherlands, the United Kingdom and the United States, have been deposited and shall come into effect with respect to other states on the date of the deposit of their ratifications.

Article 12

After the Treaty has been in force for ten years, or at any time there-after, the Parties shall, if any of them so requests, consult together for the purpose of reviewing the Treaty, having regard for the factors then affecting peace and security in the North Atlantic area, including the development of universal as well as regional arrangements under the Charter of the United Nations for the maintenance of international peace and security.

Article 13

After the Treaty has been in force for twenty years, any Party may cease to be a party one year after its notice of denunciation has been given to the Government of the United States of America, which will inform the Governments of the other Parties of the deposit of each notice of denunciation.

Article 14

This Treaty, of which the English and French texts are equally authentic, shall be deposited in the archives of the Government of the United States of America. Duly certified copies thereof will be transmitted by that Government to the Governments of the other signatories.

In witness whereof, the undersigned Plenipotentiaries have signed this Treaty.

Done at Washington, the fourth day of April, 1949.